The Only Story That Has Not Been Told About OJ

Eleonora De Lennart

Excerpt from The Only Story That Has Not Been Told About OJ

Deadly Triangle: Excerpt from The Innocence of OJ

So why would O.J. be interested in killing Faye Resnick? Something then crossed my mind. I thought, "Why is Faye Resnick pointing to O.J. as the only murderer again and again, to such an extent that it becomes obvious she is seeking to incriminate O.J. to divert attention from something much larger that must be involved in this tragedy?" (Especially because O.J. was already in jail with nobody believing his pleas of innocence anyway, so what would she have to fear?)

Faye Resnick's book seems to be sometimes illogical. (Which is surprising, considering that it has been put together and written according to Faye's words by one of the most professional writers in the country, Mike Walker.) Extremely unimportant things (like exchanging car keys, back and forth with her boyfriend Christian) received such a great deal of discussion that one can only wonder what is the agenda behind the car key story, the 911 story and other irrelevant stories— but, for example, the romance between Ron Goldman and Nicole Simpson in itself, is, except for a couple of meaningless lines, just not there.

Why would this story be more important than other love stories about Nicole? Because the whole world assumes that the trial of the century is Shakespeare's classic jealousy drama, Othello, and Desdemona. And since Ron Goldman is allegedly the reason for Othello's jealous rage, well, then at least there must be a clue for an affair between Nicole and

Ron to bring Othello into the right mood to kill. Faye must have known it. She claims that "[she] was more

into her [Nicole's] head than anyone else." "I was the best pipeline into her heart, her mind, and her soul." (55) Unfortunately, Faye Resnick left this part of the "pipeline" out. If she hadn't, we would certainly understand a lot more what was going on between Ron Goldman, Nicole, and Faye. And there must have been a story. A real story. Because Nicole, Faye, and Ron had plans, big business plans. Big plans for Nicole's, Ron's—but especially for Faye's—future. And Ron would have been the decisive factor for making her dream come true, to become a male independent businesswoman.

But Faye Resnick mentions Ron Goldman, in the whole book only with a couple of meaningless lines. And the whole story starts and ends here: "Anyway, we were sipping our cappuccinos with a bunch of the Starbucks boys, these gorgeous young aspiring actors and good-looking guys who worked out and had hard bodies," and then she goes on, "Nicole had a crush on one of them, who she thought was really cute. I agreed. His name was Ron Goldman, and the first time I saw him I told Nicole, 'There's only one boy here who's worthy—it's Ron, and he's absolutely gorgeous!' Nicole was pleased to hear my judgment."

Disclaimer

This book is the opinion of the author that is based solely and exclusively on the own words, wanted and/or unwanted, consciously, unconsciously and/or subconsciously, randomly and/or intentional statements and/or confessions, and/or accusations and/or self-accusations, narratives and/or personal experiences made by (written by) Faye Resnick, the Brown Family (in its entirety) and Goldman Family (in its entirety), O.J. Simpson, and/or their authors and ghost writers, which had been written and/or documented in their published books. They, the authors of these books and their statements, are solely responsible for their statements. While the author strives to make the information as timely and accurate as possible, the author makes no claims, promises, or guarantees about the accuracy, completeness, or adequacy of the contents of the book, and expressly disclaims liability for errors and omissions in the contents of this book.

Interpretations by the author are satire or parody, free speech and free thinking. The information provided herein is the author's opinion and provided for entertainment purposes only. At no time, will, had or has the author intended or pronounced any accusation of guilt to any author or protagonists of these published books.

Eleonora De Lennart

Look for Eleonora De Lennart's other titles
God is a Handy Excuse
The Night of the Scorpions
The BioChemical Machine 1, 2 & 3
Quinky

Introduction

It was a cold January morning in 1995. O.J. Simpson's trial had just begun, and I had no idea that I would ever write this book. I was not one of the fanatics vehemently fixed on O.J.'s innocence or his guilt. I was totally uninvolved because at the time, I was recovering from surgery and most of my time and energy was being spent on my convalescence. Deciding whether O.J. was a psychopath or the most pitiable man in America, was not my concern. At this point, I had no doubt that if he had to slit his wife's throat and that of the already dead Ron Goldman, he is indeed a psychopath. It is my opinion that he would fit into a class that includes Jeffrey Dahmer, who are hopelessly ill because of the irreparable damage their parents have done to their brains. I had faith, however, that the justice system would prevail and that O.J.'s lawyers would prove his innocence—was he innocent—or the prosecutor would prove his guilt—was he guilty.

Then I realized that most people had determined that O.J. was guilty. Every social encounter included a discussion of the O.J. dilemma. I realized that I was making enemies among my friends when I quietly suggested O.J. may be innocent and that we theoretically hold everyone innocent until proven guilty. Even my husband was convinced of O.J.'s guilt. The blood, he protested, was the convincing point and I could do nothing to change his mind. So, I gave up, especially since I did not consider it a matter of great importance. I turned it over with absolute trust to the American legal system.

But then, on one of those cold nights, I heard, by chance, about Ron Ship's testimony. He had been invited to testify on the subject of O.J.'s telling him about his dreams of killing Nicole after her death. At first, I laughed. This *is* funny. Eventually, I asked myself, "How can they allow dreams as evidence in a court of law?" If they do, surely they must invite psychologists and/or psychiatrists to assess and analyze these dreams. Because the dream, as such, has the same importance in psychology as subconscious language, Freudian slips, body language, compulsive behavior and of course, compulsive self-accusation. It is one of the basics of psychology itself. As every psychologist knows, a dream has nothing to do with soothsaying, oracles or fortune-telling. A dream is a very serious thing. Assessing dreams requires years of study and experience. Flying in one's dream does not mean that one can fly. Dying in a dream doesn't mean one is about to die in the way the dream portrayed. It means nothing more than an aspect of that person has died—he has become more mature. If we were unable to dream, we would get depressed, even sick. We need our dreams to process events. We dream about our fears, even mortal terror. We dream about our aggressions in order to deal with them in our waking life.

The interpretations of dreams by one who is not qualified, is dangerous. The assumption that something someone dreamt actually happened, is fallacious. A dream cannot be directly translated to reality. That would be an oversimplification. Yet, this fallacious assumption, this oversimplification of a complicated psychological process, was being used as evidence to convict a suspect of murder. It was difficult for me to believe this was happening in America—a country with some of the best scholars and psychologists in the world.

It was from this incredibility that my interest in knowing whether O.J. is a psychopath or the most pitiable man in America began. I knew, as a psychologist that "my feelings" regarding O.J.'s innocence has the same value as anyone else's—nil, zero. Why? Because this "feeling" is nothing but the product of one's own nervous system. It is dependent upon one's own upbringing and experience. (**[i]A1) And so I pondered where I should start. I did what German prosecutors love to do: They read the book written by the suspect (if there is one) and look for evidence. In some cases, one revealing sentence alone—convicted the suspect. Another psychological phenomenon, the compulsive self-accusation, also called compulsive confession, can play an enormous part.

Psychologists are like criminologists, that they can trace a line from the result back to the origin of the problem. They read between the lines, draw conclusions from Freudian slips and compulsive behavior, analyze dreams and read body language. They also understand the "subconscious language" which means they understand exactly what someone would not want to reveal.

I wanted to have the same success those German prosecutors had, I set out to find O.J.'s self-accusation which of course would be compulsive, unintended and subconsciously motivated. I wanted to find what the FBI calls "bragging" (of criminals about their deed), and psychologists call "compulsive self-accusation." I knew if I accomplished this, it would be one of the biggest sensations in the case. I rushed out to buy, first of all, O.J.'s book, *I Want To Tell You*; *Raging Heart* about the Brown family by Sheila Weller; and last, but not least Faye Resnick's book, *Nicole Brown Simpson*. The more I read, the more I became convinced that O.J. was not Othello and Nicole was not Desdemona, but they lived in reality (and unknowingly) the classic tragedy of "The Prince and Cinderella" which relates to "Gratitude Breeds Aggression" and the image of O.J. as the wife-beater.

In the meantime, the case was presented to the jurors, who, on October 3, 1995, within short three hours reached their verdict of Not Guilty! But this didn't mean that O.J. was innocent. Not at all. Fifty-six percent of Americans believed that a killer "got away with murder." But why would 33% consider the verdict, in fact, reasonable? Are they stupid? Don't they feel for a young man, for Ron Goldman, who had a whole wonderful life ahead? Don't they feel for Ron's desperate father whose cry of pain set his teeth on edge and caused many tears?

People couldn't believe that it was over after the verdict: they turned it (and as NBC calls it officially) into the O.J. Aftermath! The majority were simply unable to accept the jurors' decision. The comments ranged from, "We are shocked, our hearts are with the

Goldmans and Browns," to "O.J. is guilty as hell!" And they excused "such an irrational wrong decision" (of "black jurors") with "Johnny Cochran knew how to play the Race Card!" And yes, in fact, the whole case has a lot do with racism, and we all heard about the Race Card. But is it really true that Johnny Cochran convinced twelve people only by pushing their vulnerable nervous system and without facts? And what does it really mean to be a racist? What is a "Race Card" in the first place? Is it really true that someone would hate another person because of religion, skin color, gender, sexual orientation, or because they are an "Auslander" (foreigner)? Not at all.

With this book, *The Innoncence of OJ*, I am introducing for the first time the true Race Card. As a result of eight years of research, I discovered the pioneering cause for racism, namely The Breakdown of the Identification Phase with the Mother. I've established racism to be a serious illness. As well as making these important connections between, "The Race Card," "The Prince and Cinderella," "Gratitude Breeds Aggression," I hoped to find that the guilty party, in this case, would make The Big Mistake—that the compulsion would be stronger than rational thinking and would reveal him—herself. And I was lucky......

CHAPTER ONE
The Prince and Cinderella

"You just don't know what it is to be eight years old and all your friends think you have the best mother in the neighborhood," O.J. said emotionally, of Eunice, at his induction into the Football Hall of Fame in 1985. (1) "Eunice was a pillar of the community, and her values, spirituality, and resourcefulness were inspiring. Despite her week of all-night work, she was at the Potrero Hill Housing Project's recreation hall almost every Saturday night from 1949 on, helping a local minister set out the folding chairs, move the organ, and generally transform the impersonal concrete and linoleum room into a homey, makeshift church and Sunday school. In fact, she chose her exhausting work hours expressly so that she could have Sundays off to go to church. On Sunday mornings, she got up and bathed and dressed Carmelita, Truman, O.J., and Shirley, and then walked them over to the transformed recreation center for the 9:00-to-11:00 a.m. session," gushes the author, Sheila Weller, about Eunice Simpson, O.J.'s mother, in her book based on the Brown family's tales. (1)

Yes, I can imagine that O.J.'s mother, Eunice, must have been, almost fifty years ago, a beautiful, charismatic and very impressive personality, who became the center and magnetic point for many of

O.J.'s friends. Young people who needed, like all young people around the world, a role model to identify with, and who would show them that there is always hope. Young people who escaped the no-future attitude and resignation of their own homes. In Portero Hill, the San Francisco housing project, one could feel the damp fog, a reminder of the closeness of the bay. (2)

Not only O.J.'s career itself is evidence for Eunice's personality, but she was also for O.J.'s friends the one who let them forget the sad tristesse of the Portrero Hill Housing Project. Eunice would show them that even in such a sad atmosphere, where walls are often painted brown, (so that dirt won't attract attention) a glass of beer can still be half full (and not already half empty). Psychologists like to use this "beer of glass example" to demonstrate the same situation, but under two totally different point of views: the winner view and the loser view. The winner considers the same quantity in the same glass to be "still half full," the loser can also see the same quantity. But his assessment is depressed. "The glass of beer is already half empty."

Yes, Eunice was a victor—and not a victim. Her optimistic attitude was the reason why "Eunice Simpson, was indeed, the favorite mother among O.J.'s friends. O.J.'s friends from the projects—Joe Bell, Howard Rogers, and Al Cowlings—loved to hang out at his apartment. Eunice was a second mother to Cowlings," explains Sheila Weller. (1) Eunice had, too, like everybody a hard life. She struggled and fought, she has been disappointed and deeply hurt. I can imagine that she cried many tears in her life. But she showed the world—and especially their children—that there is hope and that there will always be a glass that is still half full...

"When Simpson was interviewed by Lawrence Linderman for *Playboy* magazine in 1976, Simpson put a positive—indeed, a romantic—spin on his childhood home, where, by his own estimation, seventy percent of the residents were on welfare." (3) Sheila Weller is analyzing O.J.'s interview: "According to his telling, O.J.'s childhood had a Tom Sawyer quality." I don't think so. O.J. is telling about the world that he really saw and experienced. A world created by Eunice. The world with hope and that made her unique and the "best mother in the neighborhood."

"When O.J. was sixteen, he and Al and Joe—by now this threesome were known in the neighborhood as 'The Three Musketeers'—joined a gang called the Superiors. They threw rocks at buses, stole cars for joy rides, and sometimes were hauled into the station house by the police. O.J. would set up fights, then split on A.C., leaving his friend to take the licks for him," explains Sheila Weller. (4) You almost had to join a gang if you lived in Portrero, O.J. has said. Life there was too dangerous without a group's protection. After being president of a nonfighting gang, the Gladiators, at thirteen, he moved on to the inevitable next step: a fighting gang, the Persian Warriors. "We did a pretty good amount of fighting, and the big showdowns would usually take place on holidays, when everybody would get on down to Market Street," says O.J. (4) And yet, O.J. didn't end up as a criminal, and/or as a drug dealer, which could easily have been the case.

He was intelligent, and he wanted to be somebody—because he knew from his mother that there is always a glass beer that was still half full...,And so instead of stealing cars, selling tires, spare parts and other goods—his drive was to "be somebody." He didn't believe in limitations, that the color of his skin could have prepared for his life. At the age of sixteen, he decided "to step out of all this rowdy shit and give dances instead." O.J. and his friends rented a hall in the Sheraton Palace Hotel and gave a Halloween party that hundreds of kids came to. The young "entrepreneurs" O.J., Al and Joe had perhaps their first big success/experience (perhaps even the decisive key experience) and cashed in: $ 3,300 for the night!

I can imagine, young men, holding for the first time such a vast amount of cash in their hands! Adrenaline must have flown through their bodies. Now they knew what it meant to be the "Superiors." Because, now they were superior. They proved to themselves that they made money because they're smart! Mom was right—there was always a way so that the glass of beer would be, in fact, still half full... But despite this key experience, O.J. didn't choose the classic career of a businessman who was able to make $3300 with just an idea; it was sports that became the love of his life. Sports grounded him. He was fascinated by baseball, and dreamed of being a major league catcher. (5) "But it was Eunice Simpson who steered him past the bullets of his own worst self and made him an athlete." (5)

In 1967, with the help of Wayne Hughes, a billionaire owner of Los Angeles Public Storage warehouse, O.J. made it. (6) Wayne became not only O.J.'s mentor but also a friend. In 1967 was a major alumnus from the University of Southern California (USC), and remains so today. (7) O.J. was heading for a college, and he moved out of the ghetto into the football glory. He rose from the "Superiors" and would be a "Trojan." Shortly after receiving a full scholarship, O.J. married Marguerite in a Catholic church ceremony on June 23, 1967. They moved to Los Angeles and took a small apartment near campus. Marguerite got a job as a clerk in the science library.

Simpson became the greatest football star the university had ever known. (8) O.J. Simpson had reached his goal to be SC's Trojan knight in shining armor. In 1969, O.J. Simpson was the number one football draft pick in the country, signing with the Buffalo Bills for a reported $350,000 for a four-year contract. O.J.'s readiness to fight and to win is then interpreted by Sheila Weller: "He had found a way, despite his childhood infirmity and despite his homosexual father, to win in almost every social encounter." (5)

I was really astonished about such wrong conclusions in 1995. I asked myself, what does she mean by saying "despite his homosexual father ?" Sheila Weller goes on to report in her book, based on the Brown family's memories, "A few days after O.J. beat her [Nicole] on New Year's Day 1989, Nicole said to a confidant, 'O.J.'s father was gay, did you know that? That's why he did this. I think he gets aggressive and violent like this because his father was gay." (9) I know that the Browns tried to put a psychogram together that was meant to portray O.J. as the natural-born killer personality (which he must be if he killed Nicole and Ron as was demonstrated).

Most of us grew up, believing, that the "strong father figure" is the decisive factor for a son to become a strong man. But this is exactly the wrong conclusion. The son/boy gets his strength exclusively from the mother! All outstanding (self-confident), successful, (often famous) men, have strong relationships with their mothers—and they all were "mother's boy." The names are: Abraham Lincoln, Teddy Roosevelt, the Russian Czar, Peter the Great until Arnold Schwarzenegger and Charles Barkley and many, many others (who could fill a very interesting book).

If we want to find out and to be sure, whether O.J. is a natural-born killer, a psychopath (which the majority believes) or a man who is unjustly accused then we have to analyze his mother's personality and the relationship with her son and vice versa. Nobody, except a murderer personality, is able to do what has been done to Nicole and Ron. And a murderer personality develops from childhood on. And it is the mother who can hurt her son in many ways, even by just ignoring him (as I will explain later, boys suffer more than girls). Or by leaving him unprotected to father's "strong" punishment (because she believes, subconsciously, that she is no authority for her children)—it is the mother who creates a murderer.

But O.J. was lucky. He also had one of the wonderful strong mothers who gave him (unknowingly) his self-confidence. But O.J.'s insecurity is the conflict that has been created through society about the importance of skin color. The Browns made this point very clear, "With the help of Hughes, he was heading for a college for rich white L.A. boys and girls who had grown up in the gated homes of Hancock Park and Pasadena, kids whose parents were members of no-Jews-allowed country clubs and who had known blacks only as maids, chauffeurs, and Bullocks Wilshire elevator operators." (10)

Pigmentation is only a psychological thing. It is psychological pressure to accept that it would have value. Not more and not less. It is not real because it doesn't mean anything for the quality of your brain. You don't feel it, you feel only the reaction of ignorant people who are trained to think in racist terms and really believe that there would exist such a thing like pigmentation that might be superior to another pigmentation. But as I will demonstrate throughout the book, exactly such a mirage creates a lot of self-doubt among those who have the "superior pigmentation" (like Mark Fuhrman for example, who therefore will be the perfect metaphor for my demonstration later in the book).

But why would I maintain—yes, emphasize—that O.J. was lucky and had one of the wonderful strong (original) mothers ("the best in the neighborhood"), despite the majority of people who believe that O.J.'s problems started exclusively with his father who left the family when he was five years old? Because this way of thinking is wrong. This misconception of the "strong father figure" who is the only role model and who is responsible for the son becoming "strong"—this is the root of all evil. It is the heart of most of our societal (and personal) problems. It is the reason that people are having identity problems and depression. It is the cause for eating, sleeping, and other disorders, yes, even for phobias. And it is also the cause that marriages and relationships don't work and that people create unhappy families and torture themselves through their lives. Most people don't know that they live against nature.

Many people accept (subconsciously) abstract ideas about male and female behavior because they believe that this is "normal," or at least it would be the Laws of Nature that men and women would have "their roles." But our forefathers and foremothers lived indeed for 100,000 years according to the Laws of Nature, that means the mother was not only the leader of society (in ultimate partnership with their men) but was an admirable role model that provided her sons with Identification Phase, so that he was able to develop his male identity. Therefore, our forefathers until 1000 B.C., were self-confident men (who were allowed to cry like every human being) and most definitely didn't know what hate or racism was! Why? Because their identity was so strong so that they didn't need a target that would help to divert from themselves.....

This secret, and what the reason for racism is all about, requires a full discussion. Therefore, I ask the reader to accept at this point in the book, that it *is* the case. Later, in the

"The Race Card," I will discuss in more detail *why* people are becoming racists after all.

However, Sheila Weller, who wrote the book *Raging Heart* about Nicole and O.J. Simpson based on the Brown family's memories, several times quoted the psychologist Dr. Richard Majors (Co-founder of the National Council of African-American men), who had some good theories—and sometimes my hair stood on end! First of all, he agrees to the really out-of-touch theory (then, when Psychotherapy had its origin), of "O.J.'s getting aggressive and violent because his father was gay ." Then, "In black families, there's a high degree of father absence and, as a result, a high degree of closeness to the mother. You see more role flexibility with black males—by the time they're teenagers they can cook and sew and change diapers. The father is not there; these boys have to be their fathers. They have to take care of mom. And it all falls on the mother to hold their world together." And the psychologist and the Browns go on to report, "He's [O.J.] a real mother's boy.....You could see it the day he was captured: He wanted to crawl back into the womb." (11) I was shocked and asked myself, "In which century and in which world, do these people live?" How can men and women live a happy life with such misconceptions? Misconceptions that will cripple again the minds of the next generations and will, again, remain their best enemy for the rest of their lives.

From time to time, Dr. Major comes near to the truth. For example, "It wasn't the meeting with Willie Mays that was so central to his life; it was the ongoing relationship with his mother—with a woman. That was where the energy came from." (7) But immediately after, he observed something right, he is taken by 2000 years of societal deception (and propaganda!). "O.J. Simpson may have become obsessive toward his mother—and then transferred that obsession to the other women he loved." (1)

First the gay father, who caused O.J.'s natural-born killer instincts, then boys who have to be their fathers, who have to take care of a weak mom, (mom, who obviously is unable to survive in this hard ultra-modern computer world where we allegedly and according to such teachings, still have to beat up our rivals and have to hunt for our dinner with a club) and then last, but not least, O.J. must have become, at any cost, obsessive toward his mother.

But the climax that made my hair almost really stand on end, was finally reached by the following statement: "Without a father, this son-to-mother dependence can be insupportably threatening. If there is no man for him to turn into, then who does he become? A woman?" (11) If we could trust the Brown family's and Dr. Major's psychological (thus scientific) conclusions—then there would be *no* other possibility for O.J. having developed into a gay man. As gay as his father was! This, at least, would be the logical consequence.

However, as I said, I'll discuss this subject in more detail later in the chapter, "The Race Card," but at this point, I would like to mention one simple formula: The more positive mother a boy gets, the less obsession he will develop. Quality time instead of quantity time. What does this mean? I'm sure we've all heard stories about murderers killing women who looked similar to their mothers. Yes, these are the extreme cases, of course. Rape or spousal abuse, to a certain extent, is the same psychological basis, but the illness didn't escalate to the extreme. And again, we reached the same point: it is the mother who makes her son a murderer or makes her son a hero. It is the mother who develops the brain parts via biochemical processes to be a happy person, and it is also the mother who cripples her son's mind, as, for example, in the case of the serial sexual criminal, Wesley Dodd, who didn't even know, "what feelings are to begin with," or in the case of Jeffrey Dahmer who ate his male victims (whose father stated, "God forbids homosexuality"), or Danny Rollins (who killed five people and said that "voices of demons" told him to do so).

Those 60/70% of people who consider O.J. to be a natural-born killer (a killer who was able to execute such bloody murders is beyond any perversion, and any "Not knowing what feelings are") are those who, too, must believe, that Jimmy Simpson is guilty because he abandoned is weak little wife and consequently without "the strong father's hand" the children became rotten. Of course, as it was in other cases, so it could have happened in O.J.'s case, that they would have killed each other in the heat of the moment, and by mistake.

Be it because of severe marriage problems or jealousy, but to plan a murder (which must have been the case in O.J.'s case) and to execute it, needs a real killer, (a real killer brain), that has been created by their mom—step by step, from childhood on.

If there is anything that made O.J. indeed insecure, then it was first of all the image about skin color (and its classification) and the polemic against his mother: your son is a mother's boy because you chose the wrong husband! His strong mother, the right role model for every young man, (therefore O.J.'s friends instinctively were magnetically drawn to Eunice), did everything right. It was society who made mistakes by disputing her ability to be the "Strong Mother Figure." And what is more, Eunice has been degraded exactly because she did things right! And her son, who reacted naturally (like every normal boy would react who later will be a happy man) was ridiculed to be Mama's boy.

Society dictated that she is only second class, the vessel for the semen, and that her son will be a nobody without a first class "strong father figure." There wasn't left any doubt in any reader's mind, that no gay father could provide his son with enough love so that he will feel protected. This emotional confusion, this illogical conflict, to be ashamed of the love of his mother and father, the obscenity of racism as a growing (and dangerous) cancer our societies caused O.J.'s insecurity—and that a Deadly Triangle became possible after all.....

But what is it that makes the mother so important for the development, especially of the sons? And what is it that it would be even further evidence for O.J.'s innocence? Therefore, I would like to discuss The Identification Phase with the Mother. Why is this so extremely vital for boys, and why do most of us live (unknowingly) against nature? What does it mean and what is going on in our baby boy's and baby girl's minds when the brain is still empty and contain only the basic human needs: eating, breathing, drinking, sex, sleeping? It is important because it is the root of almost all our societal problems and most of the problems that make the individual person very very unhappy.

I would like, first, explain the importance of the Identification Phase with the Mother in Dr. Bernd Nitzschke's words, "Although every child identifies with both parents at different stages, i.e. with the mother and the father, the identification phase with the mother is the more important and decisive phase for every child. Especially for the *sons*. If the identification phase with the mother is disturbed, a male child will always have difficulties with his male sexual identity." (12)

The psychotherapist, Dr. Bernd Nitzschke, goes on, "In relating to his mother, the son also acquires a female identity, which is gradually reshaped in an alter transformation process. The father, as the representative of masculinity, is a secondary identification object for his son, thus of secondary rank. If the mother fails, then, in that the identification phase does not run its course positively, her son will always remain insecure, experiencing feelings of inferiority." Every human being acquires basically, a mixed sexual identity, i.e. never a pure femininity or a pure masculinity, or as Dr. Nitzschke says, "Everyone is actually androgynous." (12)

I believe it is not exaggerated to say that the majority of people still believe in the 3,000/2,500-year-old-concept, namely, exactly to the contrary—the father is the decisive factor for the son. But this is not true. And therefore, our world is in trouble and suffers from heavy identity problems! It is the mother, who is responsible for the self-confidence and self-love of her son. The mother decides (subconsciously and often unknowingly) whether her son will become successful and happy, or will end up like Jeffrey Dahmer, Lyle and Eric Menendez, Wesley Dodd, Danny Rollins (who killed five people), or little boys who rape other little boys, or children who kill other children, or countless others—they all suffer from the same cause—the lack of the strong (and admired) mother figure.

It is the mother who cripples her son's mind like Wesley Dodd, a serial sexual criminal who did not even know "what feelings are, to begin with," or a Jeffrey Dahmer (whose father was also meant to be the role model for Jeffrey, the "strong father figure." A father who wanted to make his son "strong" with force and by any means. A father who believes indeed in attitudes like "God forbids homosexuals)."

Let us take the Menendez brothers as a further example, who are established mother and father murderers. Most people could at least understand, to a certain extent, why they would kill their cruel father. But why the mother? The mother was a victim too, she too suffered tremendously because of their father's control (because of insecurity) and dictatorship. But they killed her! The Menendez brothers explained that their "mother never took a position, and she never protected us from this cruel man"—and they pitied her. They hated their mother because they had to pity her. And she prevented them from admiring their first great love in their life—the first princess, the mother. They hated her because she failed. They hated her because she forced her sons to pity her. That means: Lyle and Eric Menendez instinctively felt the right thing, they felt the lack of something very important. Only that they didn't know (and obviously not even their psychiatrist knew), that they developed desperation and hate (and felt abandoned, because their mother prevented them from experiencing a healthy and positive Identification Phase with her! It sounds hard, but it is the truth: Their mothers made them natural-born killers.

I don't believe that anybody would assume that Eunice was a weak mother who would have been lost in this world without Jimmy, or would have, like Lyle and Eric's mother, "never taken a position" and would have been unable to stop the "strong" father figure's cruelty (cruelty is not strong). Not at all. Eunice didn't flee into alcohol or drugs. Eunice was mother and father in one person, and her son is the evidence. Because he developed instead of becoming a criminal into the most successful athlete America has ever seen.

The only problem that Eunice and O.J., in my opinion, really had, was, that Eunice (generations who experienced that women were forbidden to vote) believed, in fact, the only 2,000-year-old fairy tale that there are "women's roles" and "men's roles" (which I will discuss throughout the book). I'm sure that she didn't know that our minds are sexless and that all is individual in this world. However, one can imagine that I reacted on Brown's narratives with great astonishment. "By his third year in high school, O.J. had met a girl who would take over his mother's role in steering him straight. Her name was Marguerite Lorraine Whitley, and she was as quiet and conservative as he was big-mouthed and wild." (7) When I read this, I really laughed, and I thought "...a girl who would take over his mother's role in steering him straight?"

Which sort of identity would a woman have who consider the basis of her marriage (that should last for the rest of one's life, hopefully) in taking over the mother's role in steering him straight? Was O.J. really such a unemancipated little boy who would marry a mother-animal instead of an equal partner for life, or is this again Dr. Majors' unearthly interpretations? If he was such an underdeveloped man, who just didn't grow up, then, in fact, the beatings of his wife Marguerite must have taken place every week, at the least three times a week—out of so much frustration of so much motherly care that would choke every young person who still had their entire life ahead of them!

That O.J. didn't like this old-fashioned role, shows the reality itself. Perhaps O.J. was already at this time, one of the men, whom we knew in the 1990s as statistics show, "seventy-one percent of American men who look for a woman with personality," then they would marry immediately. O.J. wasn't to stop. I can vividly imagine that he didn't want to be buried for the rest of his life in a marriage with a wife, whose identity was to be his new mother, and who would determine what he may and may not do. After ten years of marriage, Marguerite's and his ways were already worlds apart. Marguerite was six months pregnant when the move from 3005 Elvill to 360 Rockingham began in late May, 1977. But also, a new child couldn't create new attraction and passion between Marguerite and him. O.J. was still too young to feel passionate about a woman "who took over his mother's role in steering him straight." (7)

O.J. didn't want to be steered. He had developed over the years. Already as little boy O.J. who didn't steal cars and didn't steal tires and spare parts, the little O.J., who proved at sixteen years of age that he could earn $ 3,300 with a smart idea, had grown. He had grown out of the arms of his wonderful understanding Marguerite, who steered him certainly in the right direction. But he had grown up. He didn't want a prudential match, and he certainly was not attracted to a woman who took over his mother's role. He wanted to steer himself, he wanted to be the own master over his decisions, and he wanted to live. He wanted the pins and needles of the adventure of life, of youth and beauty, of new challenges and new successful experiences. He wanted to show himself, to God and the world, that his great mom was always right—namely, that the glass of beer was still half full.....

It was only a question of time before O.J. would fall for another woman. And it was only a question of opportunity, that another woman would cross O.J.'s path. A woman who would know how to push O.J.'s bottoms. A woman who was absolutely not interested in playing mom and straightening him out. A woman who was so insecure herself, that she needed a daddy rather than a partner with all strengths and weaknesses, that every person in this world has. She needed a daddy who would take over her father's role in steering her straight. It was the seventeen-year-old Nicole, who would be provocative, challenging and turn O.J. again into a passionate man.

Nicole was the contrary of Marguerite. Marguerite was reasonable. Nicole was a sweet and exciting teenager from the seventies, but still a child. A beautiful child, who knew only her parent's attitude and way of life. Not more and not less. And at this time, it was common to believe that a girl's career was to marry. The best would be to marry money to guarantee a happy marriage. This was common beliefs. To be socially accepted, a girl had to be married. A profession and own identity? This was for average people, pretty scary. Polemics like tomboyish, Virago or other things were quickly the rumor in one's neighborhood, especially if they had bad luck with the reverend of their area who perhaps condemned such "women's suffragette's ideas" (Emanze) after all. The majority didn't like to be an "outsider," they wanted to be mainstream and accepted in the community. And mainstream-thinking is very clear: true family values are women at home, they have the children, being mothers for their husbands, who are the providers (the princes), to whom they will look up nicely, and that's it. (Nobody analyzed that life might be a little bit longer than only twenty years) And nobody had any doubt, that it is the man who must bear the whole responsibility.

I'm sure that Nicole never had been taught words like identity, personality, independency, conviction, call—in short, nobody helped her to find the way for the passion of life. If this weren't the case, she wouldn't have dropped out of high school, but she would have (her father and mother would have insisted!) gone to college and would certainly have chosen a profession that she loved (besides her family). This would certainly have been good for her self-esteem and self-confidence (and for her family). Nicole—and there is no doubt in my scholarly heart—was educated like millions of women who were trained to wait for the prince. Nicole must have (subconsciously) believed that they couldn't do more than saying, "Some day my Prince will come..." That's how she lived her life. No doubt about it. But she didn't know, and perhaps she couldn't know, that the Cinderella and the Prince concept is doomed from the very beginning, regardless how much money people have.

I believe there is no better example to demonstrate how wrong this concept is, than Charles and Diana, the most famous "Prince and Cinderella." It struck everybody more than any other example. But it helped to make the problem really transparent because nobody ever thought about the similarity of O.J. and Nicole and a million others. However, I believe, almost the entire world had seen Princess Diana's innocent glance, when she, the virgin soon-to-be-wife of Prince Charles of England, looked (from the bottom to the top) during the marriage ceremony longingly and shyly, at Prince Charming. Although she has almost the same height as Charles—she was perfect! She was blushing, obedient and submissive. That's what the future king's wife is supposed to be. When his eyes were mercifully set toward Diana, she immediately lowered her eyes. There was no doubt in almost anyone's mind around the world, that this was a perfect dream couple. One of the biggest romances of our century, right?

But meanwhile, we all know that Diana and Charles ended exactly like all other Cinderella stories, who are doomed from the very beginning because this artificial concept just won't work anymore. Many people didn't see the similarity between Diana's and Nicole's stories and those two, in turn, are again the same as millions of Cinderellas who have a regular provider with less money. But this is exactly the case. It is psychological, emotionally and practically the same old sad drama.

We human beings have one habit: we get used to everything very quickly. Even if a person didn't grow up with money, as soon s/he has money, the attitude changes. It's no longer new. And psychological problems come back, precisely those which could have been repressed during the phase of "longing for the final goal." As soon the final goal has been reached, after a short time luxury, money and whatever, loses its newness novelty. The pure naked human being is again visible—looking again for a final goal. And if there is no final goal, then psychological problems usually take over.

Regardless on which social ladder you want to establish the concept of Cinderella and the Prince, it is always the same story. Whether it is Diana, Walt Disney's animated movie, Nicole or a million unknown women—every woman who decided that her whole identity would be Mrs. Prince Charming, like it or not, are Cinderellas. "Someday my prince will come," whispers the animated Cinderella with the most innocent and sweetest look in her beautiful large eyes. And Walt Disney made it clear: it is the prince who makes dreams come true and the Cinderella who waits for the one who can make dreams come true.

"Someday my prince will come," were certainly also Diana's dreams. And she didn't only dream teenager dreams, this was her future, her consciousness. This is what she has been trained for, to behave like a woman, and to marry the right man, which could be in her case only someone more wealthy and more famous than she was herself. Her prince could be only a man that would be able to make her family more important and famous as they actually were. That's how our girls are still being trained—around the world. "Look out for a provider, a good party, marry money." That's how every Cinderella's mind is filled from childhood on. And didn't Walt Disney show us in the sweetest animated version of Cinderella ever, how wonderful a prince in love really is? He, who saved the ill-treated youngest daughter from a very sad destiny—didn't even remember her face (therefore, I guess, he needed the glass slipper for recognition). But we all understood that he, the prince, was crazy about her, even if it was only the body he fell for.

And as it happened to Walt Disney's fantasy figure, so was it certainly with Diana. When Charles proposed, she was in paradise. Charles proposing! And Diana, much too young, and not prepared for the real life, without her own identity and without self-confidence (who felt inferior to Charles anyway) would soon realize through cruel experience how wrong the Cinderella and the Prince concept was—in real life. Diana obviously didn't know better, she was prepared, and it was her understanding of her identity—to please a man. A man who can do things that she couldn't do, namely fulfill her wishes. A man who ranks higher on the social ladder. She wanted to be a good girl, the chaste girl that wouldn't be soiled by a womanizer. No, she wouldn't throw herself away, (or at least the obviously most important part). She would wait and preserve her biggest treasure for the right one. For the only one. And she would be a good mother because she always had maternal instincts. From childhood on. She was always a good girl, and now she was a good woman. (Or in Sheila Weller's words: "She would take over his mother's role.")

So, if a woman is so good that nothing can compare with this goodness— why then had this man (Charles) only one thing in his mind—to escape from this choking goodness? Diana was rich, Diana was famous and Diana was beautiful. She was admired, she had everything she wanted—but she suffered heavy depressions and an eating disorder. Despite millions, despite fame, despite admiration—her self-confidence was still zero. Her self-esteem was almost non-existent.

But here is the point, Diana didn't lose her self-esteem because of Charles, Camilla Camellia, and all these events. Diana never had self-esteem! Her self-esteem was zero before Charles (i.e. his mother), decided that she was the right woman for "his" children. And when she felt, of course, Charles' coldness, (not because he was cold, but because he was not in love), then she played, even more, the good woman, (compare with O.J.'s first wife, Marguerite, "who took over mother's role") that bored him so much. And the more he rejected her (and yearned for the self-confident and erotic woman he loved), the more she became masochistic—and less attractive.

Psychologists are much like criminologists. They are able to work backward from the outcome to the origin of a problem. Because in-between lies all the evidence—like compulsive fingernail biting, injecting one's healthy body with silicone, the choice of friends and lovers, and of course the final act, the end itself. Let me quote Professor Joachim Seidl who once said, "Nothing happens accidentally. No broken leg and no illness. No car accident and no murder. If things like that happen, then the person wanted it (subconsciously), that way, and has attracted (subconsciously) wrong and negative people, and would (subconsciously) create deadly triangles that include people who would pull one into tragic situations."

And so we come from Diana back to Nicole, our Cinderella, also a princess. Good, not with such a feudal background as Diana had, who lived indeed in a castle, but Nicole came from a small-town castle: from Lou's castle. And would she be able to dream in Lou's castle other than someday her prince will come? No, she wouldn't. We know that Nicole left high school before graduation and didn't pursue any profession or academic recognition. And we know, too, that she jobbed as a waitress perhaps with the dream of the American Way of Life.

And so during the end of the last week of June and the beginning of the first week of July 1977, "the whole group watched O.J. fall in love with the beautiful young blonde waitress on the red-brick patio of the Daisy." (13) O.J. at this time was already "one of the greatest running backs in NFL history." (14) He was not only famous and wealthy, but he was also self-confident, intelligent and optimistic. And he had the first marriage experience already behind him. One can see from O.J.'s changing idea and taste of women, that he wasn't keen to fall in love again with someone who would take over his mom's role to steer him straight. In his opinion, he was straight enough. Subconsciously, he was looking for a strong personality (like his mom) and an independent woman, a 21st Century woman. A woman with whom life would be fun and family life would be a joy. A woman with her own identity and own interests. I believe that O.J. was sure that Nicole was exactly this self-confident woman he was looking for. The kind of woman he was crazy about, (the same as the statistics that "Seventy-one percent of American men"). A woman who made it worthwhile to forget about all other attractive women out there in seductive Hollywood. And O.J. didn't know, couldn't know, that Nicole's self-confidence was based on a man's interest in her. This was her way to believe that people wanted and admired her.

But there was something wrong! O.J. noticed within a second, Nicole's unusual fingernail biting. "He noticed, as she laid the plates of food on the table, that her fingernails were bitten to the quick," explains Juditha Brown, Nicole's mother. And furthermore, "he immediately saw something in her that others would be slower to discover—her insecurity." (15) But O.J. was already in love. He would handle it, he would help her, she would stop biting her fingernails. He was a good prince, he really loved her and would make her and her family happy. And so, this time, to escape some women's ideas to be a man's mom, who would steer him straight, O.J. entered in a relationship in which he was this time a sort of daddy, namely the prince, himself.

I'm sure this felt good after ten years of marriage, especially since O.J. developed and had grown up tremendously. And so, to be the prince was new. I can imagine that he liked this role at the beginning. Because he couldn't know by which problems this role would be accompanied because it was Cinderella, not the prince, who sooner or later would be unhappy in her role. It would be Cinderella who wants to break free. And it was Cinderella who feels that she is trapped in a gilded cage! And it is Cinderella who does *not* know that she is the *only* person in this world who could decide if she wanted to fly or to spend her life in a cage. It is Cinderella who had the key to open or, lock shut, that cage. It is Cinderella that had the gilded key to open her gilded cage.

O.J. didn't know and couldn't know, when he met Nicole for the first time, that she was already seriously ill. Nicole fought against her depression and inferiority complexes her whole life. As her mother herself tells us from Nicole's childhood, it didn't change over the course of seventeen years. On the contrary, it increased. "She hated diapers and toilet-trained herself at one year. She insisted on keeping all her food completely separate on her plate at mealtime. Even if she were starving, she would not take a bite if the peas even slightly touched the mashed potatoes or the mashed potatoes even slightly touched the meat." (16)

In the 1990s, every psychologist would have diagnosed such extreme compulsive behavior with clinical depressions and would have treated her, but not in the '60s. Even if Nicole's parents would have recognized that she needed help, perhaps they wouldn't have found the right doctor. However, her attempt, years later, to seek psychiatric help (together with Faye) was in my opinion, too late. She would have needed already as a child, or at least as a young woman, a very good doctor who would have helped her to come out of this labyrinth of depression, compulsion—and as a consequence later, flight into sex, alcohol, and drugs.

Unfortunately, nobody recognized her depression as a child, as well as later when she met O.J. And because nobody recognized (or diagnosed) it, so nobody could help her. And as it is with every illness, if the illness/tumor is not recognized, it grows. No illness goes away by itself. We can use a painkiller, but the illness remains. And so it was in Nicole's case. She used her sort of painkiller and increased the dose from year to year, but the illness stayed with her and grew tremendously from year to year, from decade to decade.

Sunday, May 19, 1978, Nicole was spending the eve of her nineteenth birthday with her parents in Laguna, when all of a sudden there was the sound of two cars pulling up to the driveway. Nicole ran out, and nobody was there, just a black Porsche parked in the driveway. (17) "'Where did that car come from?' he asked, more than a little puzzled," writes Sheila Weller of Lou's reaction when O.J. Simpson parked "a black Porsche 914, with a big bow tied to its hood," in the Brown's driveway, "leaving the provocatively extravagant present for all, including Lou, to see." (18) These were the painkilling moments! When she was worth so much that a man would present a new car like chocolates at the door.

These were the great moments when she felt, for the first time, accepted and admired by her father. O.J. was the perfect prince, for the perfect Cinderella. This was exactly what Nicole's parents had prepared her for. But her mama and papa were worried. What would the neighbors say? This prince wasn't the prince they had expected, but an ebony prince. "Lou didn't have anything against blacks...He just felt that whites and blacks should try to each stay on their own side. So I figured, why don't we let this [romance] run a little bit and see what happens before we upset anybody." As we all know, Lou and Juditha made it. They overcame their aversion to "the other side" and crossed the line, upsetting their entire neighborhood.

But did they? Was the neighborhood really upset? If Nicole had married another "black guy," would he have been accepted by this family if he hadn't been a millionaire and a celebrity, but instead in Lou's own words "a bum?" (19) At least O.J. was a prince, so Lou and Juditha must have been satisfied, although they had obvious problems with skin color. Juditha recalls that Nicole once said to O.J., "'I don't know if you should be here. I'm not sure my dad is going to accept you.......Well, you are black, aren't you?' O.J. always joked about black and white, and Nicole kidded him about his thinking he was white. " (20) In every joke there lies a hidden truth! At least Nicole had something she thought was better and superior to O.J.

But as I will explain later in the chapter "The Race Card," self-confidence is a very deep thing in ourselves, that starts in fact with our parents—for boys with their mother and for girls with their father. If we don't' have this luck in our childhood, then it requires tremendous hard work for the rest of our life. And so, Nicole's snow-whiteness didn't help her to maintain her superiority, or at least her self-confidence, for very long. Soon the terrible depressions (caused by scares in her childhood) would come back.

We can assume that Nicole didn't want to bite her fingernails, that she was perhaps even ashamed to run around with ugly fingernails, knowing that many men are repelled by that, knowing it would reveal her insecurity, knowing that no man would admire her for it. Who wants that? Nobody wants that. And Nicole certainly didn't want that. On the contrary, she wanted to be admired, she wanted to be somebody—but nobody showed her how. She put silicone in her breasts because she didn't believe that anyone would admire her and love her for her personality or charisma. She thought she needed artificial stuffing in her body to be accepted. She desperately separated mash potatoes from peas—in order not to go mad because of her depressions.

But why did Nicole suffer severe depression from childhood on , which only increased from decade to decade? Which key experience was so cruel that she became so insecure and bit her fingernails to the extreme? Why would a beautiful woman be so insecure and would need to stuff silicon in her healthy body, if not for a reason?

Yes, there is a reason. Why it is so difficult for girls to heal their childhood wounds, and why so many of them end up with an inferiority (and Cinderella) complex—they lack a relationship with their father! The father has for the daughter the same importance as the mother has for the son. And by relationship, I mean a relationship. The girl that feels that her father consider her brilliant, unique—his little princess! And not, as is often the case, "just another disappointment." Nicole's lack of self-confidence started with her father's opinion of her, which was "she is just another girl." I know from a reliable source that his dream was "his son." Already blessed with a flock of girls by his first wife, Lou, yearned for his replica. My sources told me about Lou's disappointment when every yearned-for boy came out a girl, a girl, a girl and again a girl.

Nicole's compulsive biting her fingernails has an important connection to her father's lack of admiration for the little princess. To him, and according to my sources, she was no princess at all. She was only another disappointment—and of course, mother's business. Nicole never overcame her father's opinion. That Lou accepted her, years later, is another story. She was accepted at a time when she had long forgotten the wounds in her heart that her daddy had inflicted, forgotten she had learned over the years to repress that hurt. It was many years before Lou came to accept his daughter. And then it wasn't for who she was, of her own intelligence, charm, and personality. It was because she was the lover of a famous millionaire, a millionaire who could make dreams come true.

Lou was much more responsible than he thinks he is, for Nicole's Deadly Triangle. Did he send her to college? He had the money. He could have done it. Did he expect his daughter to become something special—a lawyer, an architect, a doctor, a businesswoman, a writer, an agent? Did he? Did he, her first prince, believe in her without any hesitation? I doubt it because if he had, we would know a different biography.

Why do a mother and father have so much power over a baby? Because they don't just create the baby physically, they develop its emotions, self-confidence, feeling of well-being, acceptance, motivation (you can win if you want)—or resignation (the mental block against winning). But why is it so difficult to get out of this vicious circle? Because these processes take place when we are babies or toddlers. Our mothers and fathers are molding our brain. Step by step, during the molding phase and over the course of years, our brains will store up information, like a computer chip. I use the term "computer chip" to make clear what parents can do to those billions of neurons and how they can influence the biochemical processes in our brain. And the main information comes from our parents. Their opinion of us will later be our opinions of ourselves!

Nicole probably didn't know how to escape the confusing labyrinth of her mother's and father's ideals and her real personality. She limited herself subconsciously like a bird whose wings are clipped and doesn't know why it can't fly. Nicole, (subconsciously) had planned the dependency that she hated later in life, the dependency that made her so unhappy and dissatisfied and finally led her to take drugs. Subconsciously, she chose her own sad destiny. She chose it because she believed it was all she could do, or rather, could not do. She wanted much more out of life, but accepted her parent's way of thinking, accepted the idea that she, Nicole, was unable to fulfill her dreams by herself. And this is not good for one's self-respect.

But how could anyone blame Nicole's confusion about her "role," that probably didn't suit her real personality, if we consider that a contemporary and highly regarded author, Sheila Weller, makes the following observations in 1995: "The group consisted of regular, up-from-the-working-class, self-made, sports-mad guys—and a group of women who juggled their desire to make homes and have children with these men with their need for freedom, independence, and adventure, women who rebelled from the "Boy's Club" of their "Couple's Night" life with a "Girl's Club" of their own. It is a very typical American scenario." (21)

I asked myself, "Is this the computer world of 1995 or 1795?" However, I know many men with their need for freedom and I know many women with their need for freedom! Spontaneously, I remember my tax adviser who was married to a Ph.D., she (the wife) had her "need for freedom" by contrast to him (the husband). And then there are others who are totally different. Because the brain is sexless and it is only our upbringing that causes differences in some brains (and it could be any brain, female or male). This kind of philosophy is simply out of touch. And not only out of touch, but these dangerous messages make people sick, violent, racist and depressive—because they are confused about their identity (and pressure of expectation).

However, this "upbringing" is the cause of many problems, as I will explain throughout the book. And also, one of the causes for Nicole's tragedy and failure of the marriage. Most people accuse O.J. of being responsible for their marriage. We all know the saying, "In a relationship, both sides are responsible." In Sheila Weller's book I read the analysis of Nicole's and O.J.'s confident, "Tom Mc Collum would say, 'Nicole's and O.J.'s problem was that they were so alike. They were two 'sames'.' Both strong-willed. Both confrontational. A same should be with an opposite." (22) This, in fact, is a common opinion, one I have heard from many people around the world, my entire life, "a same should be with an opposite." And it just isn't true. The only basis for a successful relationship is equality. If things are equal, then people can understand each other. And because they can feel for their partners and empathize with their experience, they will react more sensitively and with understanding, instead of reacting egotistically like we do when we don't understand our "other half." We speak of two halves, don't we?

Be that as it may, Nicole and O.J. became Cinderella and the Prince and not two equal partners, who would have made each other happy and would have helped each other. She, Nicole, was for the first time in her life, what her father obviously, had denied her as a child—she was for the first time, a little princess. And O.J., in the role of the prince, felt so strong and superior to this seventeen-year-old girl, who leaped from her father's castle into his castle. Both believed they were in control of the other—Nicole because she was the snow white princess who was superior to the ebony prince, and the prince because she was Cinderella. They were sure at least that they were totally in control of their lives, their scars, their cracks, and of course, each other and their future. They couldn't have dreamed that their relationship was stillborn and doomed to fail. Why was it doomed? Because they didn't help each other to grow in the course of those years and in the framework of a relationship that makes up for the faults of parental education. Like two children, they went on playing Cinderella and the Prince.

Nicole didn't know, couldn't have known that her depression would come back sooner or later when the newness of a princes's life wore off when the Ferrari and the mansions were no longer new. After she had reached her final goal, marriage, (according to her thrilled and enthusiastic outcry, "I can't believe I'm married!") the same emptiness came back—mercilessly. With or without wealth, it couldn't be cured by alcohol or cocaine. On the contrary, what was bad, became worse. Her depression increased tremendously along with the number of wrong people around her and entering her life.

It was as if there was a magnet growing inside her that attracted more and more negative, dangerous, and self-destructive people. Her life was filled with dangerous creatures for whom she was no match in cruelty. She wasn't able to handle them. She wasn't even able to see through them. Because these people—hopelessly attracted by the world of the rich and famous—had one advantage over her—they had learned about real life the hard way—step by step. Like Resnick, for example, who from childhood on, step by step, went from rejection to rejection, from degradation to degradation, until she finally found one man who would propose. These kind of people were hard-nosed enough to manipulate Nicole. But our Cinderella had no concept of the real world. To Nicole, the real world was either serving the king (her father) in his castle—or serving the prince who gave extravagant presents. In any case, she stuck stubbornly to her old "computer chip," the one that repeated the same program again and again and again.

When Nicole woke up, it was already too late. Biochemical processes had done their job over the course of thirty-five years, mercilessly and painstakingly precise. The vicious circle once started, became like an avalanche moving faster and faster, more and more dangerous; affairs with men became more and more addictive, but also more frustrating. She was shocked to learn that some men were more interested in the fact that she was Prince O.J.'s ex-wife, then they were in her. ("...Grant could never hear enough about her [Nicole's] sex life with O.J.") (23) She tried desperately.... She landed in the arms of Faye Resnick—and she couldn't help still biting her fingernails like a little girl—and she started to yearn for Cinderella's wonderland to come back.

So Cinderella tried to reconcile with the prince, hoping it would be the answer, the way out of her emotional dilemma, her confusion, and her growing identity problems. But it didn't work that way because she hadn't grown. She was still the little seventeen-year-old girl, who was neat and diplomatic and pleased her parents, who had no idea that sexual attraction would be the least of all reliable things in this whole wide world, and would certainly not be enough to keep a relationship happy.

The reconciliation didn't work because the spoiled prince was looking for a reason to give up his freedom for one single person in this big seductive world. He wanted a woman with personality, a woman who was attractive because of her self-confidence—like his mother. But the fingernail biting had even increased. Nicole felt more insecure than ever and became more and more upset and angry with the prince without knowing why. She felt so unhappy, so deeply unhappy. And she didn't understand why they couldn't live happily-ever-after. But most serious of all, Nicole didn't understand that the secret to everything lay inside her, that she was the only person in the whole wide world who could set herself free from the gilded cage! She didn't know that she was the only person who could heal her damaged wings, wings that had been clipped when she was still a little child. And Nicole Simpson never learned that she could have done something about her problems and growing depression, that she, in fact, could have broken free.

She just learned from other Cinderellas that alcohol and drugs would be the answer. She didn't know that drugs are only a ticket to self-destruction. The truth about her bad moods, her discontent and the conflicts with her ex-and-perhaps-future husband had a simple cause. As long as she accepted Cinderella as her identity, she would be (subconsciously) unsatisfied regardless of money, mansions, lovers, and Ferraris— and she would (subconsciously) hate herself for being thankful (instead of proud), and even more, she would hate the benefactor who made her hate herself. She would get even for his merciful bounties........because Gratitude Breeds Aggression.

Eleonora De Lennart

CHAPTER TWO
Gratitude Breeds Aggression

Let us for a moment take a closer look at the conflict which many babies, toddlers, girls, teenagers, and women have to go through. The first glance every baby gets in its life is at its sexual organs. This is in many cases for the baby girl (for eighty generations) the first experience of disappointment, and a baby's brain stores this feeling of rejection. If a girl also has brothers, then it could be that she has even worse luck. Because, in most cases, she learns the hard way what it means to be a girl. Girls must help their mother in the kitchen, while the favored brother(s) sit with daddy watching TV, or go outside to play ball. The son gets recognition for beating up the neighbor's boy, or for a fast pitch; the girl's help in the kitchen is no big deal. Because to care for the family is their "natural role."

I believe it is not exaggerated to say, that the majority of boys are praised for breaking teenage girls' hearts and are praised for becoming a womanizer. By contrast, most of the girls who are told that premarital sex is evil and sinful. Pleasure is connected to bad things. A girl has duties. The duty to remain a virgin, not to become pregnant, to be a good girl, not to be a young devil, because "a girl wouldn't do that, it's not ladylike." A girl has in many cases to be concerned about Barbie doll's wardrobe because this is the perfect sign that the little girl is a normal "female."

"Don't throw yourself away, wait for the right man." (But how could she choose an appropriate husband not having the experience necessary to establish one's own personality?) Unfortunately, in many cases, she is taught that sex will have something to do with morality. And so, since she is not prepared for the real world and not to take responsibility for her own body, for her own decisions, concerning her future—she receives the message that this thing she shouldn't "throw away" must be something like a commodity, a piece of somebody else's property.

If young men happen to be attracted to her, she very easily and very quickly gets a "bad reputation." She is a "manizer"! She is a female Casanova. In contrast to boys, who are praised for the same ability to cause attraction, she becomes now a sort of bad person. Jealous girls make up stories, and so do boys who didn't "get her." The more irresistible a teenage girl is for young men, the more she can be sure that people will speak badly of her because she is surrounded by envy and jealousy.

In cases where there are brothers, the father is absolutely fascinated by 'his' sons, who are, of course, his business. He will serve as the necessary strong father figure, the identity figure, so that his sons would become strong and do the right things in the future. Girls are the mother's business, and sometimes they are even at a disadvantage in their education. But it doesn't matter anyway, the girl will marry, sooner or later, it is her designated career.

Then the teenage girl grows up. And soon she realizes that her second-class body, the body in which father wasn't very interested, has much more value than she thought it had! The same boys who once were classroom Casanovas, are now changed. Instead of teasing her, they blush, they get insecure, some of them even go crazy. She gets love letters. Boys unlucky in love, threaten her with suicide. And slowly but surely, she gets to know a totally new feeling. This has something to do with power—an incredible feeling of power. She learns very quickly, and more, and more each year that the same body that had no value at all has now quite a lot of value. The same body that didn't interest her father is able to make all her dreams come true. And she realizes that the same body that has so little worth (even in God's eyes) can buy almost anything!

This is the discrepancy behind the folk tale of Cinderella and the Prince. This is a century old German folktale, turned by the Brothers Jakob (1785-1863) and Wilhelm Grimm (1786-1859) into the famous fairy tale, resurrected in Walt Disney's wonderful fantasy—a fantasy which is, in reality, a drama. "Someday my prince will come...," says Disney's sweet (animated) Cinderella in a sweet voice. And nobody could doubt that this is a reality. That's the way it has to be—a prince will come someday to "make all my dreams come true." This story makes it very clear that it is OK for a woman to demand and receive bounties, that this is fundamental to her identity, and that Cinderella's attitude is perfectly correct— that it's a man's duty to make sure that she will have enough bounties all her life. But, have we ever analyzed how immoral the concept of "marrying money" in itself is? I don't think so. Because until this very day, many people speak about this concept as if it is a matter of course. They speak in families, and they speak in public and in TV. They speak, without blushing, as if there were nothing wrong with marrying money.

I am sure we have all heard about trainers coaching their athletes psychologically so that the athlete thinks of nothing but winning. The winner of the Kentucky Derby in 1995, for example, called his trainer (and horse owner) the "greatest motivator" in the world. There are other cases in which athletes, although physically ready for victory, have lost because of their mental blocks for winning. This sort of training is exactly what mothers and fathers do with their little offspring. They motivate them—or rather, demoralize them!

And what is Cinderella's motivation in life? Looking for a man with status, a rich man, a name. Marry money—because you can't do it on your own. We have yet to consider how much sadness, resignation, and demoralization Cinderella and the Prince concept brings along with it. Cinderella is trained from childhood on, to believe that the American slogan "if I can do it you can do it" (and the like) is not meant for her. It is meant for her provider, whom she will choose and of whom she will make herself dependent—the man, who will be responsible for her life being wonderful or miserable. He'll be responsible for her status! Because he can do it if he wants to.

With this knowledge in her heart (and de-motivation in her mind), she sets about looking for the "right man," which she knows is a man with status, maybe money. And perhaps, if the good fairy helps her, he will even be rich and famous. At the very least, he should be a good provider, able to make her life secure by working a job, maybe several. What's important is that this whole situation becomes ideal early on, especially before the first wrinkles ruin her business opportunities, she believes.

How could Cinderella know that for 98 % of men, one of the most exciting sexual fantasies is to make love to an "older woman"? (24) How could she know that there is nothing more irresistible for most men than a woman with personality? (According to the latest statistics, seventy-one percent of the American men.) (25) How could she know that sooner or later she will hate the benefactor for making her hate herself? She doesn't know. She only knows that her only "asset" is her body. Cinderellas don't know about "mental blocks against winning," and they don't know anything about motivation—because they have never entered the race for the sake of pleasure. The only game they know is the short-sighted body game. The body is everything, put silicone in your breasts, ruin your health, don't just run around looking like a Barbie doll—be one.

Then over the course of years, Cinderella eventually learns that her body is not everything. That sooner or later it is nothing. Because she gets to know how men's love can change if they are married to this body. Especially if, from the beginning, there wasn't much more of a basis for the relationship than this body. The newness is gone, and tiring emptiness fills the room. The atmosphere is frustrating, and the woman's effort to attract fails miserably. Especially when men see the agenda behind so much effort.

And now it is often the case that Cinderella becomes more and more masochistic because she believes that pity and applying pressure, like guilt and duty to the children, will bring her man back. Because she has no other identity than being Mrs. Prince, she is fixed on him or the deadly terror of losing him, of losing her provider. And so she degrades herself more and more, and he becomes more and more disgusted while she is more and more infatuated. Her self-esteem sinks lower than ever, and he becomes interested in another woman. And so, trained to be somebody else, another identity, but herself, she learns to play the good woman, as she believed that she would "keep" her man with tricks, with silicone, with tears and fear. But playing the good woman won't work either. Aside from the fact that goodness has no sex-appeal, it must be acknowledged that in these days, no man needs a housemaid or a mother substitute.

Whether famous or wealthy, whether a true Prince Charming or only charming, these cases are all the same tragic behind the concept of Cinderella and the Prince. Because even if such women can get "divorce settlements," and mansions, and Ferraris, and

"$ 10,000 in monthly allowance," it is always the case that there are a bounty giver and a bounty receiver. Whether a movie director, a football star, a doctor, a police detective, an executive, a professor, a taxi driver, a salesman, a McDonald's employee, a CEO, a bank teller, or a small or big businessman—everybody who gives something, expects something in return. It can be money or in the form of services. But everybody who pays for something believes he or she has bought something. And if we buy something, we own it, right?

When Cinderella, attains her "ultimate goal," the wedding, she is indeed happy. Everything is fine, and nobody can understand why this paradise will sooner or later turn into a hell of conflicts. The days of the proposal and the wedding are definitely not the days that Cinderella will discover self-abnegation, which comes about only by playing (and accepting) the role society (and her mama) told her to be proper, namely being a diplomat. And which means, to renounce one's identity. Nor will she immediately see that self-denial creates self-hatred. (*A2) Who in the world could love one's own body if life had begun with such a negative response to one's sexual organs, and especially if one knew that this body sentenced them to be a servant in this world. (**A3) Think now for a moment of our athletes—who are meant to win the race, to bring glory to a proud coach or trainer. How could it work with such a bad sight at the start? It can't. As I said, all these misconceptions, invented by people one hundred generations ago who interfered with nature, are mainly the source for most of our problems—and aggressions!

But even if this misconception and training of our young people against nature is the source of most conflicts and pre-programmed an unhappy marriage, it is still a totally different situation from that what we call "domestic abuse." A wifebeater (wife batterer, spousal abuse) is a sadistic man who is very ill and whose psyche is in deep trouble. Yes, it is true. A "wife beater" is a very ill (because helpless) person and needs clinical help himself. But we shouldn't be confusing normal marriage conflicts, (that can go in certain separation phases to the extreme) who have their origin in wrong education of our girls and boys (and consequently their lack of self-confidence) with wife batterers.

Margaret Byrne, who directs the Illinois Clemency Project for Battered Women, explains "one man told his wife he would find her shelter and burn it down, with her in it." Sociologist Pauline Bart, University of Illinois states, "It's this male sense of entitlement—'if I can't have her, no one can.'" (28)

I must protest! There is no such generalization like "this male sense of entitlement." This would be unfair to men who are indeed great personalities and who are self-confident! What she means in her description (she is an expert. Consequently she must mean this) the ill man who suffers inferior pathological complexes. She speaks of the man who didn't have the luck to go through the vital Identification Phase with the Mother to establish his male identity and his self-confidence! She speaks of the man who suffers castration fear, and the so-called "original fear of man" to fall in love with a woman, and who suffers pathological fear of being abandoned. She speaks of the man who fears woman's erotic power and his being at her mercy. She speaks of the man who hates in every woman his mother!

A wife-beater is a very weak man. There is no doubt about it. He is a fearful man. No doubt either. In most cases, he becomes an alcoholic. And his psychological disposition is, in fact, similar to those extreme cases who rape women or kill them (sexual crimes). It is well known, that they chose victims who resembled their mothers in some ways, be it the way she spoke, acted, or physical similarity. And then the hate grew to the extent that they couldn't control themselves anymore.

"Mother, mother why have you forsaken me!" This is the true cry of pain behind every sexual murder, rapist or wife-beater. This is the true cry of desperation of men who (unwantedly) lack the development via biochemical processes of certain parts in their brain, that, if not developed as a child, will be lost forever. They didn't have the chance to feel, to love and to admire their mothers when they were little boys. And they will suffer the same negative relationship with women for the rest of their lives.

But let us discuss the illness "wife-beater." Interestingly enough, we can discuss cases from Europe, Arabia, Japan, and America—they are, according to my studies, all the same. There is psychologically no difference, they have all the same cause for their illness, and all men are clinically depressed. They *all* have serious problems with their mothers and the lacking Identification Phase. And there is no difference in behavior: They *all* have *no* friends, no social life. They *all* live in isolation after they come home from work and they enjoy their prison (and to be the jailer). And they *all* have obviously only one goal: to control their wives and children. Because this is the only place on earth where they can put the balm on their inferiority complexes by having artificial moments of physical superiority. Here, I agree with Margaret Byrne and Pauline Bart, who have developed pathological insecurity, behavior disturbance, and inferior complexes that can only trigger in, "If I can't have her, no one can."

Let us take, just for example, the case of Adolfo Tobar, who killed his wife Jolanda in a small California town for reasons like, "her hair was more important than taking care of him," or "her mother cooked instead of her." If she didn't obey his order to cook by herself, he threw a temper tantrum. At the end, he stabbed her with a knife because she didn't obey and accept him as her master and lord. Adolfo is, by the way, able to "explain the Bible in detail, but he is obsessed with women and sex." (29)—And he had no friends.

Hamid Al Raja, a teacher in Medina (Saudi Arabia) locked his wife up for one year. She was not even allowed to speak to (female) servants. He put dark paper on every window and wrote notes throughout the house how stupid women are and how much he hates them. Neighbors heard her screaming three to four times each week because he beat her up. And he had no friends! He didn't even talk to neighbors, which is very unusual in a town of Medina. Neighbors speak to neighbors in Medina, make friendships and visit each other frequently. And last but not least, the case of Michael Buchta, German Engineer, and alcoholic, who has beaten up his wife every week to compensate his inferior complexes and the frustration caused by his boss. Not only that he lost his job sooner or later —he too had no friends.

Because they have no friends, (because they don't want friends), they are behavior disturbed and live isolated, (are often alcoholics—because of their illness, not reversed!) they project their obsession-hate toward their mothers to the new target: they project their mothers onto women. They hate any similarity to their mothers (but they choose subconsciously exactly the same type as the mother so that the game of "torturing Mama" can go on and on for the rest of their lives...)

The Brown family reports "Nicole's voice—it would be the only time the American public heard her voice—literally quivered with fear. Simpson's behavior during this now-famous 911 call is something that the white and feminist communities view as a prime example of nascent domestic violence, but many black males see it as a case of a man shooting his mouth off at a woman whose behavior with another man has brought disrespect upon him." (30)

It is true that the O.J. Simpson case has shown how dangerously America is divided. It is not only black and white, yellow and religion, militias and government, but it is also becoming worse: it is male against female—it is female against male! And this is dangerous. Because men and women are the cells of society. The cell of the families, the cell for our happiness and for our future. And a cell eaten by hate? It can't work. And why would I defend O.J.? Because it shows the hysteria of all groups. I am a simple humanist. I love men and women alike (or I dislike them), but a man can't be condemned only because he is a man. This would be the same as it happened with women for hundreds of years, who were prosecuted and called "witch" only because they were women. Thirty million women were tortured and murdered. Most of them were the doctors and scientists. But yet, we call them witch!

It is my personal belief, that, if we, the human race are so hardened (and dehumanized!) and don't care for one human being anymore, we will not care for hundreds or thousands of people. And such an attitude is in our age, pretty dangerous. An age where were we *have* to get along in only fourteen years with the double of people (namely ten billion)—if not, then it will happen as scientists like Professor John Holdren stated, that we are on our way to "extinction and self-destruction." (31)

I believe that O.J. is innocent. I don't know him, and if I were convinced that he is a wife-beater, I would recommend him to go to a good doctor who should treat him. But he has a mother like Eunice. She was able to show him that she is the victor—and not the victim—of a man! He admired her, he loved her, and she was there for him: strong and powerful. And she is the reason why O.J. became O.J. No, O.J. doesn't hate women. His mother didn't breed this sort of hate. She didn't cripple his mind. Not in a million years. He doesn't live isolated, and he has friends and a social life. He has no inferiority complexes, perhaps the sort of insecurity, as everybody (even the surest person) can have, especially while falling in love. No, O.J. even made it to overcome psychological problems that our societies create because of the image of skin color. There is no psychological presupposition that causes the illness "wife-beater," except the lack of the Identification Phase with the Mother. It is just not right to point at one "target" (O.J.) that has been chosen to be our "wife-beater" of all wife-beaters, by ignoring all facts. This is not justice. And justice is, according to our scientists, equated with having reached "subjective consciousness."

O.J. is not Othello, and Nicole is not Desdemona. Their marriage problems were pretty average. O.J. (as a man) is a normal man, who had normal marriage problems with a woman who must have believed in woman's roles and man's role. She believed that for a woman, the most important goal is marriage and children. And if she would feel differently, then "something is wrong with her." Unfortunately, she didn't develop to become an independent personality over the course of seventeen years. She didn't grow in the relationship. That means: a positive relationship is that both help each other to develop—very often away from their parents' old-fashioned way of thinking. Nicole remained all her life the sweet little girl from the 1950s, that needs a daddy. Nicole's problem was that she didn't overcome her parent's view, namely her Cinderella-identity.

However, to manifest O.J. as the wife-beater of all time, the Browns are telling their view (and they share their view with most feminists) in their book that "it would be the only time" the American public heard Nicole's voice. But this is not true, because I heard Nicole saying, "There was no beating for four years." (32) She was giggling and flirtatious. One could hear, Nicole was happy. Nicole and O.J. are flirting while talking about this one event. And, "Uh, we went our separate ways." (33) And it was recorded on one tape. And it was the only time that this tape has been aired by CNBC or any TV station after all.

But let us turn the time once again ten years back to February 1985. Nicole was still happy and in heaven, because she reached her ultimate goal which she believed would make her happy for the rest of her life. The great dream she had dreamed for seven years finally came true. "I can't believe I'm married!" Nicole screamed, overjoyed after she and her prince had exchanged vows and rights. "I'm married, I'm married!" Hundreds of guests, socialites, famous names, and reporters, as well as her mother, father, and sister, were there, and all were part of O.J. Simpson's elegant wedding celebration that made Nicole's dream come true.

"Who is this woman who won her way into the heart of this intelligent self-made man, this charming womanizer, this funny entertainer who was not only welcomed at every party around the world, but also into every Cinderella's heart?" This could have been the question. And the answer. "She's a regular girl, nothing special, just a nice old-fashioned girl." As for all old-fashioned girls, the wedding was also Nicole's "big day." O.J. was Nicole's trophy. After all, she had conquered a man who was not easy to conquer (seven years considering a marriage is, in fact, a long time), a man who was not only famous, but a man who himself knew best that he could get almost any Cinderella he wanted. He didn't even have to do it like Prince Charming, who could only identify the right Cinderella by the tiny glass slipper she had lost fleeing the royal ball at midnight.

No, Nicole's and O.J.'s love story didn't become Shakespeare's Romeo and Juliet, or Marc Antony and Cleopatra, not even Othello- and Desdemona. It became the same old Cinderella and the Prince story, that just won't work anymore in today's world, and certainly not in the seductive world of Hollywood. It's the story of the one who gives the bounty—and the one who receives the bounty. "O.J. was generous to a fault with Nicole. She got an allowance of somewhere between $5,000 and $7,000 a month, and O.J. showered her with gifts. They owned homes in New York City, Beverly Hills, Laguna Beach and San Francisco. And they constantly jetted off for deluxe vacations at resorts in Florida, Aspen, and Mexico," writes Faye Resnick. (34) Allowance? Can any grown up person in the world live with something like an "allowance" (think of the root of the word to allow) without getting depressed?

I know that many won't like the question that I'm raising now. But to make things conscious so that important societal changes will take place (slowly but surely), I risk making some enemies: Was this marriage also O.J.'s "final goal"? Has he ever mentioned his wedding as the pinnacle of his life? Did he ever say that Nicole's "saying yes" was the fulfillment of all his dreams? Or did he beg Nicole for seven years to marry him? I don't think so. O.J., the prince, loved Nicole, his princess, in the way that he believed would in fact, be love. So, why shouldn't he marry her?

But, as it is for an average man, so it was also for O.J.—once he had proposed, his duties had begun. The sweet little blonde teenager Nicole, came up with ideas similar to Marguerite's. She, too, wanted to take over his mother's role in steering him straight. It was again not the joy and beauty of equal partnership that O.J. was looking for, and again he was expected to become another person. Step by step, O.J. was presented with conditions. "We were talking about O.J.'s not true blue," says Kris Jenner (then Kardashian) in Sheila Weller's book. "[Nicole] said that he had really promised to turn his whole life around...He promised her that he wouldn't cheat on her anymore— that after they married, he would be faithful." But I have never understood, don't understand, and never will, how anyone can force anyone else to feel something. And if it is so hard for a woman or a man to be faithful, why marry? But on the other hand, studies confirm, that men and women who do love themselves and have their own strong personality and identity, are the ones who are able to love others. (35) Due to their self-confidence, they usually don't pressure their partner with fear and jealousy, and are, if they decide to enter into a relationship, in fact, faithful (voluntarily).

I believe that also Nicole subconsciously feared, like all insecure women without their own identity, that O.J.'s interest in her was limited to a short-term attraction. I believe that she knew that on every corner stood another Hollywood beauty and that O.J. was not always physically crazy about her. "You don't know what it's like to be O.J. Simpson. I have women all over me. They put their telephone numbers in my pocket. What am I supposed to do? Say no?" (36) Perhaps she knew that sexual attraction was the least of all reliable things on earth. But what would have made her really attractive and irresistible? Her own identity, her own interests, and consequently her self-confidence. And so I imagine she was rather concerned about what if the prince left her? What could make her more attractive than others?

Perhaps she knew that there was something to the old saying, "the best sex is after a huge fight, because then comes the famous reconciliation." But the fights came naturally, anyway. The more depressed she was, the more this culminated in violent anger, and the more she attacked O.J. as a consequence. Perhaps Nicole believed that creating conflicts was the only way to show strength, to cover up her feelings of inferiority, and to distinguish herself from all the other beautiful women with beautiful breasts and beautiful blonde hair and silicone in sunny California— the only way to say to Prince Charming, "I don't need you. I'm so sure of myself." But she knew he would return.....at least for a while, and at least as long he didn't really fall in love with another woman.

I'm sure many will object when I maintain that there is no true love between the Prince and Cinderella. But they were, in fact, an interest group, and that's what held them together. They both had a reason for choosing the other party. Both of them based their emotional lives on a total misspeculation and miscalculation. O.J. probably believed that he fulfilled all of Cinderella's dreams, because he laid present upon present at her feet—Porsches, Ferraris, and whatever—put her in a castle (the mansion), even made her mama and papa happy before the marriage, by making the "Ritz Carlton Hotel a second home ," or by arranging a business career for Nicole's father, who could "take over the hotel's Hertz rental agency." O.J. fulfilled his duty completely and made his princess satisfied and happy—and expected her to be grateful in return! (37) But this was not the case. She wasn't satisfied, and she didn't feel gratitude at all. On the contrary, the more her joy—to which chocolates in the form of Ferraris and Porsches were connected to gratitude—the more her aggression increased.

"How is this possible?" many will ask. She had everything she wanted, and she was discontented. Our Cinderella was just too human. She had everything her teenageheart once yearned for: a wonderful mansion, an apartment in New York, housemaids and nannies, gardeners and limousines. And what is more, she had fulfilled society's expectation, she married. She had reached her final goal and must have realized that there was no other goal to reach. To experience this at the age of twenty-six is, in fact, depressing. The people surrounding her (and her growing conflicts) couldn't understand it, and especially her husband. Didn't he fulfill all her wishes? Didn't he even include her mother, father, and sister into his family? Wasn't he a truly good prince who parked a Porsche "with a big bow tied to its hood" in her daddy's driveway to impress the entire neighborhood?

Yes, of course. She knew that nobody could understand her depressions even her so-called "relief depressions," her inactivity, her strange sadness, and her growing insecurity. And she knew they were right. But even though her friends and family could not feel her pain, she felt nevertheless a terrible emptiness. (**) She was desperate. She couldn't even describe exactly how she felt. And she knew that no logic in the world could justify her feelings. So let's sniff a little cocaine, or let's have a drink. It was sophisticated anyway. It was chic. It was in. And Nicole wanted to be "in." She wanted to be like Faye Resnick, who knew how to treat arrogant men.

But what is it? What is depression? And why would someone like Nicole become depressed, especially since she now had everything? As I said, the 100 billion neurons are very independent of money. To them, neurons are key-experiences, childhood experiences, traumas certainly more important than a red Ferrari or white Porsche. People who suffer heavy depression are often extremely sensitive, but most certainly haven't overcome their childhood traumas. They suffer pathological insecurity, regardless of how successful they become later in life. As I said, it often happens to be that (especially) women, as long as they were busy seeking the final goal, had something to divert attention from themselves. And the same old sad story happened to take place in Nicole's life. Once the ultimate goal had been reached, the real problem started for her—there was nothing more with which she could have repressed the wounds in her computer chip, her mind. As I said, she needed clinical help when she was a child (and compulsively separating peas from mashed potatoes) but even more then, approaching the first magic number in life, thirty.

Perhaps Nicole had a lot more potential than she realized. However, as we know from the Brown family, for seven years Nicole's ultimate goal was to become Mrs. Orenthal James Simpson. What came next? She had everything money could buy, and she also had the socially admired status of a married woman! "I can't believe I'm married." A rich and a famous husband. And she even had legal rights, so that her future was financially secured. But despite this paradise, the fingernails biting didn't stop, the alcohol didn't stop, the drugs didn't stop—on the contrary.

"A half-hour rampage ensued......O.J. did what he had done many times. He walked up the stairs and threw down Nicole's framed photographs of her family," says Denise. (38) The photographs served as the symbol for the cause of the problem. Apparently, O.J. felt instinctively that there was the source of the problem. He, too, must have had a hard time understanding why such a beautiful woman, whom he loved so much, went on biting her fingernails compulsively, now that they were married and she had no reason to be nervous.

But what he couldn't know was, that those depressions were unhealed childhood wounds, the first bad sight in her life, the lack of recognition for being "a brilliant girl," the lack of her first prince's admiration for being his adored princess. And he couldn't know that Nicole shared this feeling of self-hatred with the other thirty-eight percent of American women, connected to self-denial. O.J. is no psychiatrist or psychologist. He couldn't know that Nicole's computer chip was just repeating, and repeating again the sad old story of suffering, of second-class status, of looking for a more capable person than herself, the story of dependency, of receiving bounties and saying "thank you", and not having much worth in this world. Even as some would say, "But Nicole was worth Ferraris, mansions, millions, whatever she wanted?"

There is nothing worth more in this world than the personal "success experience" based on one's own capabilities. To fight and to win! To prove to oneself that one is unbeatable. That's pleasure, and that's what gets adrenaline pumping through the body. That's what makes one attractive because it lets self-confidence grow. And from there starts what we call charisma. To hunt for bounties can give only very short adrenaline rushes because saying "thank you" will be the consequence. And gratitude doesn't make for adrenaline—but for aggression. Slowly but surely, it causes discontent, psychosomatic illnesses, conflicts, and worst of all—depressions. (**A4)

People who suffer depressions, suffer in different ways. Some get quiet and live it out—" the forward depression." Some people express their aggressive feelings toward themselves in uncontrolled and unexpected attacks on others. But one thing is sure, everybody who is depressed suffers tremendous torment. The chemistry in our brains just isn't working properly. Therefore, I am not surprised when Nicole's family said: "What may be most apparent from the incident is how Nicole could push things with people to the edge. And not heed warnings." (38) The books about Nicole, talk about her violent anger and temper tantrums, her "equally provoking" participation (39) and her "confrontational" personality.

Yes, Nicole was the classic depressed personality who transforms her self-hatred into violently angry attacks. All of Nicole's positive energy, which she could have transformed into something successful, something she might really have loved, something that would have helped her to recognize how much worth she really had in this world—all that energy she put into the marriage, devoted it toward the target husband. And her husband couldn't understand why he became the target of aggression? He believed that he was a good boy and that she had everything she wanted. But since she had reached her ultimate goal (and in Nicole's case we know that there was no further "ultimate goal" suitable to our modern world) so the violent anger got more violent, the boredom got more boring, and the emptiness got more empty. And the husband (in this case O.J.) stood there and didn't understand anything anymore—and fled to his good old friend and tried to relax away from all the stress, whose cause he was unable to comprehend.

One problem caused the next, and the problems accelerated. The prince believed he had done everything right, and fulfilled his duty—which meant for him that he had not only duties—but also rights! The most important right is the right to have nothing changed. And that means, whoever has the money has the power. She wanted it this way. Didn't she? Didn't she know the formula of our modern world— "Independent and free, or dependent and unfree?" And that this is an unwritten law? And didn't she know that a combination like "dependent and free" just won't work? (Remember that seventy-one percent of American men would marry immediately a woman with personality). Why didn't Nicole's parents send her to college so that she, the teenager of seventeen, could learn something that would be her fulfillment and her existence for the rest of her life? Then she would have been free all her life, and if she had loved O.J. nobody could have stopped her from marrying—but the marriage would have existed on a totally different basis, the basis of equality, and so by fairness.

Didn't Nicole know that one day she would hate her benefactor, especially once the final goal had been reached? Didn't she know that one day she would suffer (and hear from her own employees and friends) that she was only Mrs. O.J., and that one day, she would hate being Mrs. Orenthal James Simpson, as the Austrian nanny, Gabriella, witnessed? (40). Didn't she know that she would learn how it feels when friends come to visit only because of her husband, O.J., and not because of her? Or as it happened much later, after the divorce, that lovers were not even interested in her personally, but because she was O.J.'s (ex)-wife? (41)

Nicole wanted to break free, this is true. She tried to find her way out. She tried to get her wings in shape to start all over again. But she didn't know how. And she couldn't know. She didn't even know what true wings looked like. Wings that had been clipped when she was a child and her brain could be molded in any direction. The glass of beer could have been still half full—forever. And since she never learned to fly and to do things on her own, and thus didn't (subconsciously) respect herself, how could she handle a true breaking free from someone who had been her benefactor for fifteen years? She couldn't. She did what many women in her place are doing—they want to be free, but also want their husband's wealth.

It is said, that O.J. treated Nicole like his prize possession and was possessive. (42) And I don't' hesitate to believe these narratives of family and friends. Because, every man, and every woman in O.J.'s shoes, around the world does the same, has always done the same and always will do the same. O.J. paid. And everybody who pays believes he bought something. But there is a truth, that's the same for all people— "independent and free or dependent and unfree." Nobody can be both, dependent and free. (Respectively, of course, one can, but then shouldn't be surprised about the conflicts that are created by such unequal partnership)

However, I wouldn't be surprised, that increasing depressions led Nicole to seek as much sex as possible, and to prove to herself, by sleeping with other men than O.J., that she was irresistible—to create the pseudo-feeling of "being alive." And also the psychological reality for many people who often seek conflicts and quarrels (with an ex, or unfaithful partners) "better negative contact than no contact at all." That means, they create situations, (and of course they know for many years how to push the buttons of their counterpart) so that they will release their aggressions in physical arguments. *The Inquirer* story mentioned the 1989 battering charge against O.J., the one O.J. screamed about in the famed 911 tape—the one that was played on TV and radio stations after the murders. In that tape, O.J. raged about the oral sex Nicole had performed on Keith Zlomsowitch in the middle of the house, according to reports because he was concerned about their children.

Nicole's problems with her depression must have accelerated tremendously. The gruesome, vicious circle is—drugs and alcohol interfere with the chemistry of our brains. That means the more one drinks or take drugs, the more depressed one becomes, and the more insecure one becomes. And the more insecure one gets, the more alcohol and drugs one consumes. Perhaps she believed, like I have experienced in similar cases, that divorce (at least as a new final goal) might be the solution for her increasing dilemma. Perhaps she would feel better, free again? And often it is the only hope that she could start all over again. But Nicole's depressions grew, mercilessly, from month to month, from year to year, from decade to decades—because she didn't know why. She didn't know (and couldn't know) that all this had only to do with the computer chip in her mind. She could escape from O.J., from Grant, Kato, Keith, Joseph, Ron, and the Starbucks Cafe boys—but she would never be able to escape from herself.

For someone who is not self-confident, reaching thirty is reaching one of the magic numbers in life. It is an age that nobody believes they will ever reach. What will the future bring? Is it over? What if men aren't attracted to her anymore? Is she still sexy? These are the burning questions, and this is the age when depression easily increases. Because who should she ask? Someone who struggles even more to get a grip on her psychological problems like, for example, Faye Resnick? One who can overcome this dilemma only by taking drugs? Unfortunately, she was not wise in the choice of people around her during this new phase of her life. Subconsciously, due to her insecurity, she chose mostly the wrong people. And with the wrong people, one goes into a downward spiral. Slowly but surely. Faye's power over Nicole obviously grew. So-called "Safety-boxes" arose (in which evidence for divorce settlements have been hidden), which demonstrated to Nicole even more how much she was indeed "male dependent" (as Resnick calls it). Nicole's self-esteem must have sunk below zero. Alcohol, drugs, and boys—meant to be her painkillers.

And the prince? Conflicts between O.J. and Nicole increased. Yet, like every prince, also O.J. couldn't handle the problems that every Cinderella has, sooner or later. The prince believed indeed that having married Nicole, having fulfilled her wish, would mean living happily-ever-after. According to Juditha and Lou Brown themselves, (at least during the first interviews after the murder, before they changed their mind about O.J.'s innocence), O.J. was a wonderful son-in-law. Like most men in similar situations O.J. also believed, he, the old-fashioned prince, didn't deserve such bad treatment. When I add up all the stories told by Nicole's family, I realized that O.J. did the same, as many others do in the same situation, he paid her back. But I mean by that, O.J. paid Nicole back the same way as many people handle their emotions. Chaotic. Childish. Back and forth.

If you ask me about O.J.'s motive for killing his ex-wife, then I will answer: From the psychological point of view, O.J. had much more satisfaction annoying the living Nicole and her family. There is no doubt in my mind that it was much more satisfying for O.J. to pay them back, for what they had done to him, much more amusing than killing Nicole. O.J. did things that demonstrated to Nicole "that she was nothing without him." To torture Nicole with the IRS, to feel her and her dependency—this caused most certainly orgiastic feelings for O.J. The feeling of power and superiority. Who would give up such salt in the soup of life? Denise Brown recalls, "Anytime he had anything to drink, he'd start picking on her. He'd say, 'You don't look good.' Or 'Look at your fingernails. They're all bitten down.'" And Denise said to O.J. ".......You treat her like shit." (38) It is only human to keep up the status quo. It will only change when one day the true new love comes into one's life, only then do such relationships end forever. But this was not the case with O.J. and Nicole. Take the famous IRS story, O.J.'s cat and mouse game with Nicole. Nicole "owed the IRS $90,000 in capital gains taxes" (43) (because she put down the Rockingham address on her tax return, and hadn't bought another property for business purposes.)

"The bombshell dropped the next day. A letter from O.J.'s lawyer arrived. It restated O.J.'s threat, this time in legalese. This message was clear: O.J. was going to call the IRS and turn Nicole in for tax fraud.' Nicole exploded! I had never seen her so upset, so furious," writes Faye Resnick. (44) "If you don't realize how wonderful I am to you, then it's time you learned what real life is like," reports Faye Resnick from this event. "I want her to be in as much pain as possible. Without me, she's nothing. Let her live in reality for a while, so she'll appreciate how good she had it with me," Faye Resnick quotes O.J. in her book. (45) How could a dead Nicole "live in reality for a while?" And how could O.J. have the benefit of observing with pleasure how she "would appreciate how good she had it with" (him)?

O.J.'s pleasure was to prove to her, every second, every minute, every day, that she needed him and was nothing without him. And he had a very unfriendly way to prove it. Because only $90,000 were left from the divorce settlement. This she would now have to pay to the IRS, and so she would need him more than ever. Unfortunately, our subconscious is often doing exactly what it shouldn't be doing. This is why we pick precisely that partner "who sees in us what we see in ourselves." And according to Nicole's sister, Denise, we learn what Nicole saw in herself, namely that he treated her "like shit ." (38) As it is in most cases, so it was according to the evidence with O.J. and Nicole. The more submissive Nicole acted, the more annoying O.J. became. The more Nicole needed O.J. and tried to be quarrelsome, the more O.J. teased. As I said, I believe that this game could, for O.J., have gone on and on and on—but not for Nicole and her mother and sister. And this is understandable.

But to blame O.J. for Nicole's behavior, would be the same as blaming him for Nicole's compulsive separation of peas and mashed potatoes, as well as the rest of her compulsive neurotic behavior and clinical illnesses. Nicole would keep this pattern, choosing men who were attracted to her for a thousand reasons, but not for her personality. Because her first prince and the first love in her life had made it unmistakably clear that she had no great value, that she was a disappointment—and this lack of self-esteem stayed with her for the rest of her short life.

The problem is that women who have this childhood deficit and whose longing to be loved, are never satisfied, and unfortunately, confuse making love with love. Because women like Nicole lack self-confidence, they believe that sexual attraction is in fact attraction. And through flirting and feeling attraction, they come to know what their fathers have denied them—they feel self-worth, they feel "wanted." The need to attract a man becomes a sort of addiction. It is often accompanied by addictions like eating, alcohol or drugs. And a woman's consumption of sex, drugs, and alcohol intensifies. As with any addiction. Slowly but surely.

Nicole and O.J.'s relationship was far from over if they continued to act against each other, to tease and make each other angry, to flirt and have affairs with Paula, with Brett, Grant, Keith, Ron and even Faye. It went back and forth. They were addicted to each other's vexation. It was like salt in the soup, pepper in their daily lives; it was even a consolation to know they still meant something to each other. And the decisive point was: neither O.J. Nor Nicole had found the new "great love of their life" and thereby broken the emotional ties, making it possible to bring the relationship to an end in an adult manner.

And in the midst of all of it, was the famous gratitude—that just wasn't there! O.J., the party with the money, believed like everybody in his shoes, that the other party will appreciate what he has done for Nicole and her family. But this, too, is wrong thinking. From both sides, from O.J.'s and from Nicole's. And so, Nicole and O.J. continued their childish game. Today he got on her nerves—tomorrow she annoyed him. Today he took revenge on her, tomorrow she paid him back. Both knew the other's weaknesses. Though they were free to have affairs with other people, they were nevertheless in a certain sense, still together. Faye Resnick confirms this by quoting O.J. with the intention to debunk him. She claims that he said about Nicole "Without me, she's nothing. Let her live in reality for a while, so she'll appreciate how good she had it with me."

I read in the Brown family book, written by Sheila Weller, as well as heard many times, that O.J.'s statement "I'm sorry, I'm sorry" is the admission of guilt. I disagree. I believe that he meant by this "I'm so sorry that I teased you, I'm sorry that I left you alone with dangerous people around you." Perhaps O.J., who might have suffered at this very moment, the greatest pain of his life, having lost his beloved princess after seventeen years, in such a tragic way—perhaps O.J. felt sorry that he had teased and tortured Nicole in her last days in their last childish power game with the IRS as his instrument of childish revenge.

I personally would have, indeed, reacted that way. But, perhaps, I can say this, because I experienced the death of someone very close to me and whom I also hurt very much. And I reacted exactly the same way. He died when he was only thirty-five years old. An age that nobody would expect anyone to die . But it happened, and it was too late to take anything back, or at least to resolve the pain I had caused. O.J. himself, writes in his book this desire "....to resolve with the Browns.....," because there are "....so many unresolved issues with Nicole that I'll never be able to resolve with her now that she's gone." (46) I believe that he felt responsible for having betrayed Nicole by not protecting the little seventeen-year-old Cinderella from a very evil fairy, as he normally would have. This , in my opinion, is the reason that O.J. writes in his book, "Its a fault of mine. I now find it a fault. I know in my heart that the answer to the death of Nicole and Mr. Goldman lies somewhere in the world that Faye Resnick inhabited." (47)

Let us turn the clock again back to the time when Nicole was still alive. One can see the dangerous changes that had taken place after Faye Resnick's entrance into Nicole's life. Slowly but surely, her life took a totally different path. Perhaps this new idea of life was even against the will of Nicole's mother and sisters because it seems to be very unusual for the Browns (who have displayed a great love for details) to mention Faye in only one short sentence, i.e. Nicole's "partying" with Faye Resnick.

However, Faye, the ultimate Cinderella, opened for Nicole a totally new world—who knew exactly what had to be done to get rid of the stigma of being "only Mrs. O.J. Simpson." Starbucks boys in Nicole's sports cars, big plans for business, "the restaurant thing," (48) the cafe, Jeff's driving the Ferrari, Ron's driving the Ferrari, "doing him", man-hating, becoming "finally male independent", the golden cage—these are all totally new attitudes for Nicole. Attitudes that Nicole-Cinderella had never known before. She didn't even know she could keep all her treasures—even without the prince. And she learned, with the help of the experienced divorcee-Cinderella, that little "safe deposit boxes" can turn one into the owner of Ali Baba's miraculous treasure mountain.

And Nicole learned from Resnick, something very new indeed: that the body of a woman in her thirties is worth even more than the body of a seventeen-year-old Cinderella. And she learned that an old Cinderella is even more powerful than a young one, that she has legal rights, she has lawyers, and that in this world of showing off about divorce settlements, every year means cash dollars. How much is her divorce settlement worth? Ah, she is worth ten million. No, Ivana was worth much more. How much? Twenty million.

However, Cinderellas like Faye Resnick, are fixtures in the world of the rich and famous. Whether you meet them in Paris or Rome, St. Moritz or Munich, New York or Beverly Hills, they are all the same. They think the same and they act the same. And those I know or studied their cases, are all just as dangerous. When I read about Faye's business enterprise, meant to make them "finally male independent," and I thought, here lies the problem, (and secret) of every woman who "married money" and is trying, (after having reached the goal) to be then again male independent. When Faye left her mother, a nurse, and started out in life, she made her money exclusively with the help of men. If this hadn't been the case, then we would see today a totally different biography of Faye Resnick. But we don't. After a divorce settlement from Paul Resnick, a wealthy businessman, Faye, by her own admission, had at the time of Nicole's murder, only $ 20,000 left and was unable to pay for her share of the proposed Starbucks (or rather Ron's "restaurant thing," his dream) (49) which she hoped would make her, according to her own words, "finally male independent ."

So, when I studied the strong influence Faye Resnick had on Nicole, I pitied Nicole. In my opinion, she just didn't realize what a mess she was getting into. Because it is a totally different thing to enter into the business world and to earn money the hard way, step by step, over the course of years, so to say, the old-fashioned way, from "dishwasher to a millionaire." Today, in a world where everything is available, where everything is organized by multinationals, to start a successful business isn't an easy task. And no doubt, as soon as two socialites like Faye and Nicole try to start a cafe or a restaurant, there are already expectations. They have to come up with something special, or at least with something that "Mrs. O.J. Simpson" and "Mrs. Paul Resnick" can make competitive with other enterprises in one of the most luxurious and expensive places in the world.

I must admit, I was amused when I read that Faye wanted to become "male independent" with $20,000, trying to do something that would easily require the investment of half a million dollars. And I don't believe that other L.A. princes, banks or investment groups would put their money in a Faye-Resnick-enterprise without Paul Resnick's and O.J.'s financial involvement and bank guarantees. But Faye, as well as Nicole, already had problems. They had almost no money left, at least not enough to start a competitive cafe or restaurant. O.J. was teasing Nicole with the IRS so that even this amount would have vanished. This annoyed Faye to the extreme. And both Faye and Nicole were approaching the next magic number—forty—which made them probably even more nervous. So this time it had to work. They must become rich, at any cost and at any price.

Ron believed the promises of these two women who (as we can read) thought they had to impress young men, the "Starbucks boys." They thought they had to be finally male independent—bigshot businesswomen—by promising that they could finance "Ron's dream, the restaurant thing." Just so! In Beverly Hills, in the most expensive area in the world, they wanted to set up a little cafe, or make Ron's "restaurant thing" come true. But for this, they needed a lot of money. Hard cash. Half a million dollars.

I wouldn't be surprised if Faye Resnick were the driving force behind Nicole—a dangerous driving force. Because people like Resnick are very good at one thing—they know how to bluff. According to my sources, her entire life is based on bluffs. She bluffed with the Beverly Hill's society using a self-invented biography, a family background that never existed. She bluffed with Paul Resnick, she bluffed with a lot of people—and she bluffed with Nicole.

How could a person like Nicole not believe in somebody like Faye Resnick? How could Nicole have doubted Faye's knowledge of this world? Nicole, who leaped from her father's castle into O.J.'s castle, who had been protected her entire life—until Faye Resnick came into the picture. Nicole had no time for introspection, no time to think about her past, present, or future. If it wasn't her sisters who wanted to party, then it was certainly Faye Resnick, whose first question must have been, every day, like Cinderellas around the world, "what are we doing today, where's the party?" Because the party means free food. There are millions of Katos and Fayes who live this way. And live pretty well. But to be a houseguest was certainly not Faye's ultimate goal. I assume that she believed that much higher things must have called her. Producing gym-videos with Christian Reichardt's money, (but talking bad about him) or doing Ron's restaurant thing, without Christian's money. Making millions, and kicking out people herself, instead of being kicked out by Camille in Beverly Hill's indisco "The Gate." I wouldn't be surprised to learn that's what Faye's dreams were all about.

And perhaps from there, from Faye's dreams and clipped wings and Cinderella tragedy, her abnormal desire for admiration and yearning about being "finally male independent" started a deadly triangle, that included not only Nicole Brown Simpson, who was magnetically attracted from so much self-confidence of Faye's, as well as must certainly have impressed Ron Goldman, who cannot have believed otherwise, than that he would be, finally, also a lucky dog in California.

But as sad as it is, Nicole is also another example of how the mental block against winning (created in childhood) attracts subconsciously the wrong people—exactly those people who will destroy them one day. Because this *is* the mental block against winning—to become the never-ending victim. First, from the parents (who are demotivating their children, often unknowingly!), and then after being used (subconsciously) to being the victim and not knowing the cause, they chose subconsciously the wrong girlfriends, the wrong husbands, the wrong boyfriends, the wrong business, the wrong business partner—and they trust the wrong people.....

Nicole didn't have enough time to digest childhood traumas and to get rid of such a dangerous blockade in her mind. Nicole remained all her life, a child with a parent figure around her, whom she believed, would make the right decisions. Juditha was the first parent figure in Nicole's life (and in Lou's castle) when she was still a child or teenager. Later came O.J., although a prince with his own castle, it was still Juditha who was the responsible parent figure. "I was so close to Judy that I talked to her more than Nicole did. I tried to find answers to what Nicole may have been dealing with, or going through, what was weighing on Nicole that she couldn't express to me," explains O.J. himself (50). Yes, I can imagine that Juditha, the queen of Lou's castle was responsible for both children: for Cinderella and the Prince.

But despite Juditha's personality, Faye Resnick's strong influence over Nicole and her decisions, grew. Perhaps Nicole believed (as many in her situation would believe) that it was the way to cut the umbilical cord and to establish herself indeed as the person she always wanted to be. A persona with her own identity and self-esteem. But there is no doubt, years of development lacked in Nicole's life— at least from age seventeen to twenty-seven. The years to make her own experiences. Years in which young people have to complete their education, to establish themselves as an independent identity with a profession and future, long before they will be able to choose to share their life with another person.

But the lack of those years would cause the direction that Nicole's fate would take one day. Because it would again be a dominating parent figure, she is used to trusting all her life. It would be Faye Resnick, a strong person who would make the decisions for Nicole. How could she know what was right or wrong? She couldn't know. Because she never learned to be her own decision-maker. She, the little girl with dreams and hopes, was surrounded by so many decision-makers all her life, that she did not even have a choice. And all these decision-makers knew that Nicole's temper would need "no warnings," and that could "push people to the edge." In reality, the attacks of violent anger were the increasing outcries of desperation.

But Faye Resnick understood her, Nicole believed. And it is true, Faye understood, in fact, Cinderella's woes. Faye Resnick was there for Nicole and her "girlish" talks. And Faye Resnick gave her advice on how to get rid of husbands and showed her how much fun life could be with young men and houseguests. And she was active, she planned a cafe or a restaurant—and she was so sure of herself. She didn't even care to be kicked out from time to time. And Nicole was impressed, believed in friendship and had again had the situation she was used to from childhood on, somebody else to be the decision-maker. (**A5/A6)

We will never really know, but perhaps this time she was serious about starting a future with a man in equal partnership. To build up something together with Ron—as a life and business partner. But unfortunately, she was no longer the young teenage girl that would be giggling with another girl about "girlish" games. This time, the decision (or *not* making the right decision) ended in The Deadly Triangle.....

(**) all "quotation marks" made in this chapter indicate statements made by Faye Resnick (except as indicated otherwise).

CHAPTER THREE
The Deadly Triangle

If Lyle Menendez had only kept his mouth shut, the infamous Menendez brothers would still be at large. They certainly wouldn't have become infamous, and the case would still be one of many unsolved cases. But one of those brothers couldn't keep quiet about the "weight that restricted [his] chest." Lyle felt compelled to bare his soul and accuse himself in front of the trusted authority figure, his psychiatrist, and so spelling his own and Eric's doom. Despite that, they didn't even suspect at the time, when one of the brothers confessed the gruesome murder to his psychiatrist. Lyle Menendez didn't have the chance to write a book, instead of confiding in the psychiatrist. Why? Because the Menendez brothers were at this time, still not, the Menendez brothers, who would be interesting enough to entertain the crowd.

And so Lyle Menendez's medium for the compulsive self-accusation was not a written statement, but his psychiatrist who reported it to the police.

But Faye Resnick, -Nicole Simpson's companion, was already in the center of attention at a time when she felt the same way as Lyle Menendez, suffered the same "weight that restricted her chest," and was overwhelmed by the same driving force to accuse herself compulsively. What would a heroic deed be worth if nobody knew about it? Nothing. At least not for neurotic people. And compulsive self-accusation is, as the implication compulsive indicates: neurotic.

Faye Resnick was lucky. Her authority figure, Mike Walker (comparable with Lyle's psychiatrist),was a man whose only interest was to sell millions of books, and get the sales figures of *The National Inquirer* to rise and rise. No more and no less! He wasn't interested in revealing secrets. His only interest was, "Girl, tell me all so that we can make a couple of .' million." And 'girl' told all. But 'girl' hadn't enough time to think. And so Faye Resnick didn't think about what would happen, if one day there would also be a psychologist among her readers, who would read her book, *Nicole Brown Simpson*, and find out about her hidden secrets and traces that led to the murderer of Nicole Brown Simpson and Ron Goldman. I guess, she didn't even know that there was a phenomena like 'compulsive self-accusation' (or compulsive confession). She just talked and talked, happy that an authority figure would voluntarily listen to her—and even pay her for talking. This was new, quite a sensation and made her obviously incautious.

Whether Lyle Menendez made an emotional confession to his psychiatrist, (the missed father figure whom he could trust) or whether Faye Resnick told Mike Walker, (the missed father figure whom she could trust), who then wrote a book—it is, in the final analysis, the same. If Lyle Menendez had been at this time in his life, already the famous Lyle Menendez, would he too have been able to control his emotions and have confessed in disguise—as Faye Resnick did?

And if Faye Resnick wouldn't have been at this time of her life, already in the center of attention, for which she yearned her entire life, she too would have reacted like Lyle Menendez whose "chest was restricted by the weight" and would have told someone the whole truth behind a story that we call The Trial of the Century, so that she would get into the center of attention. Why would she do this? Let me answer with Professor Joachim Seidl's (**A7) words: "These people suffer an abnormal desire for admiration. They will do anything to become famous. And if that doesn't work the easy way, then they try subconsciously to become infamous with the help of a scandal. It's better than nothing! An extremely religious background breeds a guilty conscience toward society, and therefore the compulsive self-accusation occurs subconsciously." He goes on to explain, "These people do get the disapproval of society; if they cannot achieve positive respect then negative attention is better than nothing."

Or as the FBI man, Joe Wells, calls the phenomenon among criminals, the compulsive self-accusation due to the abnormal desire for attention. "Sometimes they brag." (51) Whether these feelings and emotions are then lived out with bragging, compulsive behavior, and negative attention, they are all connected to extreme feelings: Feelings of hate and love, of rejection and disappointment, feelings about what the mother did, feelings about what the father did. Feelings of abnormal desire for admiration and show off, feelings of inferiority, impotency and yearning for superiority. Feelings of envy, jealousy, and greed. But also, a feeling of finally having triumphed—the yearned for victory!

But also, a feeling of guilt, that in one way or another, wants to be digested. But how can feelings of guilt combined with feelings of victory, be absorbed and digested? Such a chaos of emotions, and a malfunctioning of brain chemistry. Can anyone do this alone? Probably not, because besides all those deep emotions there are other feelings, simple feelings. Feelings that we "must" urgently share our good news, great joy and happiness with someone. We can't keep it to ourselves. The need to share is nearly compulsive! Sometimes our emotions are so overwhelming that we are "dying" to tell someone in great detail about the emotions that excite and stir us. These are the feelings which we have to imagine if we want to understand the impulse to compulsive self-accusation.

But sometimes people are caught up in extremely dangerous and life-threatening situations so that they will do anything they can to keep quiet and they will do their best to forget any sort of guilty conscience for the rest of their lives, and just try to survive. But whether they like it or not, the emotions remain. Overwhelming emotions. And sometimes the emotions are stronger than they can bear. And one of the strongest emotion is the yearning for victory!

This desire is especially strong for those who suffered inhumanely as children, whose souls have been deeply injured from childhood on, and who have therefore developed an abnormal "desire for admiration, "due to their chaos of emotions and malfunctioning brain chemistry. This abnormal yearning for admiration and the orgiastic feeling of triumph caused not only Alexander the Great's downfall, but also Napoleon's and Hitler's. It is the same impulse that subconsciously made Timothy McVeigh drive his car so fast that the police caught him (so that society could pay him its negative attention.) It is just as much at work in the case of Eric and Lyle Menendez's or as the FBI calls it "sometimes they brag." (51) And of course, it plays an important role in the Trial of the Century.

"O.J.? Compulsive self-accusation? Did he finally admit that he did it?" many will ask. No, O.J. is fighting for his life and for his 100% not guilty verdict. I am talking about the most controversial figure in the whole Trial of the Century, I am talking about Faye Resnick. I can hear people laughing, as everybody does if the subject comes to Faye Resnick's dark involvement in Nicole's and Ron's death. "The theory of drug dealer involvement is ludicrous," many will say. Is it really ludicrous? What makes the majority so sure? I know that almost everybody wants to know who really killed Nicole and Ron, and why. Almost everybody wants to know the motive for the murder and which kind of man would murder and decapitate other human beings in execution style. As well as many want to know whether Othello killed Desdemona in a fit of jealousy. Right?

This is almost the last part of our journey, and I show you how you can sneak into other people's minds, how you can find out whether they are lying, or whether they are trying to cover up things, you will find out the truth about what they are telling you—subconsciously and unwantedly. Namely. exactly this, what they do *not* want you to know. It's a sort of tool, how you can lift a curtain and look behind the scene. And you can use it in your own life, and you can use it in the O.J. Simpson trial.

It is Faye Resnick herself who gives us all the answers for the truth in her written statement, in her book, that was published two months after the gruesome murder. Of course, I know for myself, that exactly *this*, namely the truth, is *not* what she wanted us to know from her written statements. She wrote and wrote, and did everything to convince us that O.J. is the only guilty party in this deadly triangle. But she couldn't control her subconscious. Because she didn't know. She didn't know that her written statement would be a sort of "El Dorado" for psychologists and psychiatrists, who are, as I said, like criminologists. Resnick did everything to divert us from her involvement in this gruesome murder. She exaggerated and pointed to O.J. as the cruel animal because she knew that most of the people will believe her.

But exactly Resnick's exaggeration in her book made me suspicious! She portrayed O.J. not only as the obsessed Othello, but much worse—as King Kong, the dangerous animal who is not only obsessed with the white woman but seems to be a natural-born killer, as violent as an enraged animal who has nothing else in his mind but killing Faye Resnick. If O.J. were, in fact, the man who killed his ex-wife in a fit of jealousy, then he would indeed be Othello. (**A8) No doubt about it. But this Othello wouldn't be interested in killing any other person than Desdemona herself. He wouldn't be interested in Faye Resnick at all.

Her explanation for O.J.'s intention to kill her had become very simplified. Namely, her "life is in danger [because] of what I know." (52) Meanwhile, I have become curious, and I really wanted to know what she knew that was so dangerous.

Why she had reason to believe that her life was threatened by Robert Shapiro and O.J.'s "powerful allies," as she calls them. (54) Because in my opinion, everyone knew about O.J.'s and Nicole's marriage problems.

So why would O.J. be interested in killing Faye Resnick? Something then crossed my mind. I thought, "Why is Faye Resnick pointing to O.J. as the only murderer again and again, to such an extent that it becomes obvious she is seeking to incriminate O.J. to divert attention from something much larger that must be involved in this tragedy?" (Especially because O.J. was already in jail with nobody believing his pleas of innocence anyway, so what would she have to fear?)

Faye Resnick's book seems to be sometimes illogical. (Which is surprising, considering that it has been put together and written according to Faye's words by one of the most professional writers in the country, Mike Walker.) Extremely unimportant things (like exchanging car keys, back and forth with her boyfriend Christian) received such a great deal of discussion that one can only wonder what is the agenda behind the car key story, the 911 story and other irrelevant stories—but, for example, the romance between Ron Goldman and Nicole Simpson in itself, is, except for a couple of meaningless lines, just not there.

Why would this story be more important than other love stories about Nicole? Because the whole world assumes that the trial of the century is Shakespeare's classic jealousy drama, Othello, and Desdemona. And since Ron Goldman is allegedly the reason for Othello's jealous rage, well, then at least there must be a clue for an affair between Nicole and Ron to bring Othello into the right mood to kill. Faye must have known it. She claims that "[she] was more into her [Nicole's] head than anyone else is." "I was the best pipeline into her heart, her mind, and her soul." (55) Unfortunately, Faye Resnick left this part of the "pipeline" out. If she hadn't, we would certainly understand a lot more what was going on between Ron Goldman, Nicole, and Faye. And there must have been a story. A real story. Because Nicole, Faye, and Ron had plans, big business plans. Big plans for Nicole's, Ron's—but especially for Faye's—future. And Ron would have been the decisive factor for making her dream come true, to become a male independent businesswoman.

But Faye Resnick mentions Ron Goldman, in the whole book only with a couple of meaningless lines. And the whole story starts and ends here: "Anyway, we were sipping our cappuccinos with a bunch of the Starbucks boys, these gorgeous young aspiring actors and good-looking guys who worked out and had hard bodies," and then she goes on, "Nicole had a crush on one of them, who she thought was really cute. I agreed. His name was Ron Goldman, and the first time I saw him I told Nicole, 'There's only one boy here who's worthy—it's Ron, and he's absolutely gorgeous!' Nicole was pleased to hear my judgment."

And without any connection to judgment, cute, and hard bodies she writes immediately the next sentence, namely after her judgment was heard: "But looking back on it, I feel a lot of guilt. I don't know why, and I know it's irrational. Nothing I did cause[sic] [She wrote 'cause' without the "d"] Ron's murder. But it's just something that will bother me forever." Obviously, it was easy for her to cope with her feelings of "guilt," because she forgot immediately about her grief and went on without any transition to write: "Let me answer the burning question, once and for all: Nicole and Ron Goldman were not lovers. No matter what you've read in the press, no matter what speculation has intrigued you, it's just not true. What is true is that, inevitably, Nicole was going to "do" Ron. It was something that was going to happen. But Nicole was in no rush."

But at this point, and before I go further into analyzing Faye Resnick's written statements about her involvement in this murder case, I would like to remind you that Faye Resnick and Nicole wanted to do 'Ron's restaurant thing,' (which I will discuss later in this chapter). That means they wanted to establish with Ron Goldman and Nicole Simpson, a big business enterprise in California. Since this is no big secret, everybody knew about it— even the Browns— that means a lot of talks were going on. Faye must have known Ron very very well, and not only because Nicole considered him "really cute." And not only as superficial, as she tries to make us believe that "Nicole was pleased with her judgment" (55)—but because they were planning a big business.

Although she writes almost two pages only about her car-key-exchange with Christian, and she writes painstaking details, throughout the whole book, about her panic, fear, oral sex, lesbian sex, and then her dramatic flight from Othello (but left Desdemona home alone), as well as many many pages that seem to be exclusively written for those to whom it may concern—you can read almost nothing about Ron Goldman!

Ron Goldman must have played an extremely important role in Faye Resnick's life, but she doesn't talk about him in more than a few lines. Why would Ron Goldman have played such an important role in Resnick's life, more important than her fiancé Christian Reichardt? Because Ron Goldman's restaurant thing was supposed to make Faye, (in her own words) "finally male independent," and this was Faye Resnick's biggest dream and desire. Nicole and Faye would have been unable to make Ron's restaurant thing without Ron. Why? Who would have run the business? Nicole and Faye would run the show, but Ron would do the hard work. From early in the morning until late in the night. I am sure he was ready for this. Ready, to make his dream come true—the restaurant thing.

Ron must have also believed, that the two socialites would come up with the money they would need for this enterprise, and he would have worked, day and night, with all his strength and all his heart, for a good future. One must try to imagine how a young man feels when he meets two beautiful women, who knows how to play the game. Women that behave rich, live rich and spend money as if they were rich. Because they are used to spending their husband's money for years. And so was it with Ron Goldman. He saw a mansion, worth millions of dollars, he saw the provocative red Ferrari, was even allowed to drive the Ferrari. Ron Goldman saw two big spenders, namely Faye and Nicole. I am sure that he didn't even think about that they might have financially no background at all.

Nicole and Faye knew that "something bad was coming." Nicole had even made her last will a month before dying—there must be some truth to the fact that they both knew "something bad was coming." But did Ron Goldman also know that something bad was coming? I doubt it. He was just a man who believed that he had conquered two great socialites. That he, too, was one of the lucky guys in California who would make a career, could make his dream come true: his own restaurant or his own cafe! (*A9)

Party here and party there. Red Ferrari here and white sportscar there. But according to Faye Resnick's written statement, she had no relationship with Ron Goldman at all. Allegedly, she didn't know him much more than through Nicole who was "going to 'do' Ron." (55) But when did such meetings, talking about the business enterprise, take place? When did they talk about money? How much money was Ron Goldman supposed to invest in this enterprise? Or was it discussed between Nicole, Faye, and Ron that he would invest his physical work instead of cash? (Which in real life is often the case) How well did Faye, her future business partner, know Ron Goldman? The Browns were already informed about this enterprise. That means it was discussed openly, it was talked about, and it means that there was already much more to it than just Ron's dream.

Has Ron's death, i.e. Faye's "guilt"- something to do with the financing of this enterprise? Why would she have to feel a lot of guilt at all? Even if she feels grief, that doesn't mean she is guilty of anything! What would be, in fact, her guilt?

Especially why would she have a guilty conscience about Ron Goldman if O.J. is the murderer?

Does she believe that Ron should have fled with her together from O.J. to Kathy Harouche's house, Christian's house, back and forth, leaving Nicole home alone? And why would she have all these strong emotions only for Ron Goldman and not for her beloved best friend, Nicole Simpson, who according to her own statement, was also her lover? These are all questions which need to be answered.

"Nicole was pleased to hear my judgment. But looking back on it, I feel a lot of guilt. I don't know why, and I know it's irrational. Nothing I did cause [sic] Ron's murder...Let me answer the burning question, once and for all: Nicole and Ron Goldman were not lovers," Faye wrote, as I said, in the middle of writing about gorgeous men, hard bodies, Starbucks boys, pneumonia, a birthday, O.J. dropping by flowers and presents, cocaine and its insidious grip, shopping and kids, and Nicole's thinking about whether Ron Goldman was "worthy" or not.

There is just no logical connection to this grave and important statement about feelings of guilt—except she knew Ron Goldman much much better, as we know, and that there is indeed a reason for a guilty conscience. Why, otherwise, would she have the same emotions as Lyle Menendez (the discrepancy between triumph and guilt) who couldn't live any longer with the pressure and the weight that "restricted the chest?" Why would she have to defend herself with, "Nothing I did cause [sic] Ron's murder"? She says so because there is (subconsciously) reason for defending herself.

Why would she need to emphasize anything of this sort in her book of sex, sexual potency, lesbian encounter, sex with candle light and sex without candle light, Nicole doing Ron, Nicole doing oral sex on Keith, Ron being Nicole's lover or not. Why would anybody have to write—without any connection to the statements before or after—"I don't know why, and I know it's irrational. Nothing I did caused Ron's murder. But it's just something that will bother me forever." (55) But as I mentioned before, this exactly is what happened. To me, it looked rather like a very thick spot of black and evil ink, (in Faye's words) that something that will bother me [in fact] forever.

I knew immediately that there was something wrong—something very wrong. And immediately I recognized that Mike Walker played at this very moment the role of Lyle's psychiatrist. Resnick subconsciously opened her heart. She didn't tell him the whole truth. Of course not. With such tales, she could have relieved herself of a lot of pressure, the weight "which restricted her chest." But since any wrong word could possibly cost her not only her freedom, but perhaps her life, she would be a fool to tell anyone the whole truth. To murder another human being is, in fact, the ultimate act of control. To take a life means to have power. It means to be master over life and death. You don't have to be the one who actually commits the murder. Just being involved as an accessory to the crime, generates a great deal of excitement.

But there was in black and white, on page 185 of *Nicole Brown Simpson*, Faye Resnick's own admission, in her own words, that she had something to do with the murder of Ron Goldman! Otherwise, she would have felt only the deepest pity and sorrow for him *and* for Nicole. She certainly would not have a guilty conscience. Why should she?

Once I had made my discovery, I started to read Faye Resnick's book all over again. Everything that I read before, now took on a totally new dimension. Things that I hadn't noticed the first time, now jumped out at me. Yes, I found her hatred and her King Kong version of O.J. pretty exaggerated, but I hadn't realized, while reading this book for the first time, that this was obviously just a cold calculation with a clear-cut purpose, to reach those to whom it may concern.

As I said before, psychologists are like criminologists, they can trace a line from the result back to the origin of a problem. They read between the lines, draw conclusions from Freudian slips and compulsive behavior, analyze dreams and read body language. And they understand the "subconscious language," which means they understand exactly what someone would *not* want to let the world know. Reading Faye Resnick's book again, I discovered a lot of inconsistencies, illogic's, contradictions, and compelling self-accusations and all of a sudden, it became clear to me that this book was not an ordinary book about Nicole and her lesbian encounter with her allegedly best friend. I saw that Faye Resnick's book is much more. It is the key to the truth. Not only did she write in her book "To whom it may concern," but after having finalized my analysis, I believe the book is meant to be in fact a message—To whom it may concern.

And so, come with me and do what I did, read the book thinking of it as a message—"to whom it may concern...." (57), and I realized that this message is meant to save her life. To do this using a book is a very smart idea—as she writes herself, it was her lawyer's idea. First, she can make some money with it (and be "finally male independent"), and second, there are no wiretaps, no telephone surveys, and no moody witnesses who later "have dreams." Most of all, Faye Resnick can tell those people "to whom it may concern" exactly what she did in the D.A.'s office. She can publicly protest "bizarre defense gambits."

She can even communicate to her friends what she wants them to say so that they won't make any mistakes—later in court. She can tell us frankly and openly what she said in the D.A.'s office, what she didn't say, and what she never will say. Above all, she can make sure that those people whom she fears know one thing for sure—that she will do everything to have O.J. hanged and she will be as silent as the grave.

I saw in reading Faye Resnick's book that unimportant (and boring) stories written in painstaking detail serve an important purpose, and that other stories (which might be much more interesting for the reader) are often mentioned only in one short sentence that is might not even notice. But the message itself will be strikingly clear "to whom it may concern."

I realized that the motive for the murder must have something to do with "photographs" and "journals," perhaps with blackmailing somebody with photographs, and with the danger that one's identity might be discovered. Perhaps it had something to do with secretly shot photographs, and perhaps even with the same old "girlish" game: to collect evidence in a "safety box." Faye Resnick likes to use the word "girlish," and from there we can conclude that she perhaps, in fact, didn't see the difference between a simple divorce settlement and the drug world. My feeling was overwhelming that the motive behind the murder might have been the naive games of two women who didn't know exactly how much danger they were in.

"Fine, " one can say. "but Nicole made her will one month before she died." (58) And I agree, it's quite obvious she felt, like Faye Resnick, that "something bad was coming." (59) But Nicole didn't need to make her will to protect her family from O.J. as some people believed, with whom I discussed this striking point. Why would she? She was already divorced. And Resnick didn't have a man she could "lean on," a man who could have helped her out—because her men perhaps didn't even know! Christian, her boyfriend, just called her "paranoid" and who knows, perhaps had just kicked her out. In the days before the murder, Faye moved from Christian's to Nicole's house, then moved out of Nicole's into Kathy Harouche's house in Beverly Hills—because O.J. was after her, as she explains. Then she moved from Kathy's house back to Christian's and finally into a clinic. (60) And all this was driven by her mortal fear.

But let us start with the "photograph" and "journals" story. Faye Resnick writes in her book, "To the professional thieves-for-hire who stole personal journals and photographs from my home in the wake of the O.J. murders, I say: 'Attempts to intimidate me and silence me have only strengthened my resolve to write this book. Your invasion of my privacy and the placing of phone taps at my home have literally put me in fear for my life. I have no doubt about who sent you to steal my property. The only journals you stole were those covering the time period leading up to the murder of my best friend, Nicole Brown Simpson.'" (61)

Some pages later she writes again, "...certain pictures and documents mysteriously disappeared from my home." This time I was bothered by so much accuracy and by the effort, she made to inform those who had stolen the journals (and knew exactly what they had stolen) that "the only journals you stole were those covering the time period leading up to the murder of my best friend, Nicole Brown Simpson."

Then it became confusing because after saying that someone allegedly sent "thieves-for-hire" in order to "put me in fear for my life" and made "attempts to intimidate and silence me," Faye changes her mind a couple of pages later and lets the world know that the same evil people "...never explicitly threatened me." What? Who hasn't explicitly threatened her and who has? Those to whom it may concern? Or Robert Shapiro? Faye goes on to write "to whom it may concern" that "O.J.'s head lawyer, Robert Shapiro, had quickly surmised where I stood on the question of O.J.'s guilt, character and conduct as it related to a possible motive for Nicole's murder. And when they realized I would not be testifying for the defense, they put on the pressure." (57) Faye also says, "I know that powerful allies of O.J. Simpson will do everything in their power to discredit me." (54)

"Marcia Clark hadn't said a word in response to my plea for more time before I made a statement. I leaned forward and tried again. 'Marcia, I mean what I said, I'm not trying to get out of doing my duty. But O.J. knows what I know. That's why I feel that I might be murdered." (62) And then she communicates via the book what Marcia Clark's timing will be. "'...It's not necessary for you to make your statement right away...We'll be talking soon.'" Those to whom it may concern fully understood and didn't worry at all.

I came to realize that tremendously strong emotions play a huge part throughout the book—hatred and jealousy, rejection and frustration, man-hating and male independency. And I saw that Mike Walker was obviously the father figure she had yearned for all her life, a father who finally and for the first time in her life, would listen. A father who would look into her eyes and say, "Girl, you can trust me, I am the good prince. I will make you rich and finally male independent, you can tell me everything you know."

One must imagine, Faye Resnick, who for the first time in her life, has made her own money due to Nicole's death, and who felt for the first time in her life, important. But this wouldn't mean that the computer chip in her mind would have changed. She was always tough. She hardly escaped her parent's labyrinth only with this mentality. And now she was finally there where she always wanted to be: in the center of admiration! I recalled the psychological point of view about the abnormal desire for admiration and the desire to show off. And it became clear to me that she would never ever give up this yearned for "male independency," that she reached with the help of O.J. Simpson and Nicole Simpson.

And I felt that she would never tell the truth. She would never help justice to prevail. She would sacrifice everybody who could end her newly reached paradise. Because parts of the brains of such people were damaged when they were still little babies. But Faye, as many others too, had bad luck with her mother and father, who created a computer chip that from childhood had been programmed with evil, evil, and more evil. "My childhood was practically one long lecture on the evils of drink, drugs, and most of all, sex. I sometimes wonder how may women's marriages were ruined by parents who brainwashed them to believe that sex is dirty and evil," explains Faye Resnick. (63) (I ask the reader to recall the importance of a religious background in case of compulsive self-accusations). She speaks about herself, how she was brought up as a Catholic and then became Jewish. She suffered tremendously for her mother's way of life and the brutality of her father, who even spanked her for bed-wetting.

Yes, Faye Resnick must have suffered tremendously, living in her parent's milieu between "sex is dirty" and the punishments of God. Her parent's house wasn't a mansion of the rich and famous. There wasn't a swimming pool, not even a boat with servants who could serve a "Bloody Mary" while she sunbathed. There was no Jacuzzi and no personal decorator like Warren Sheets, "who knew more of my most intimate secrets than my husband" (64), and who would "research [my] lifestyle" for more than a year. There were peanut butter sandwiches, spaghetti, and Faye Hayward's big dream, just to get out of there— any cost and at any price.

I can vividly imagine that she clenched her teeth, believed in Walt Disney, and knew that there was only one way to escape the smell of the kitchen: to become Cinderella. Only Cinderella could buy with her body the kind of luxurious life, the boats, the mansions, and the millionaires that Faye had in mind. Far away from the punishing stepfather whom she hated. She was right to hate him because he (besides her mother's worshipping him as the strong father figure) caused without a doubt Faye's extreme hatred for men in general—as well as her abnormal desire for admiration.

Because she never had succeeded in pleasing her father! If her father didn't consider her brilliant, intelligent, and sweet, how could other men see this in her? She was not the little princess for the first prince in her life. Faye never learned that she was worth being loved and adored. She only learned bad things about men. That man can't be trusted.

Her first father figure beat her because she did 'bad things' out of desperation. Children wet the bed because they don't feel loved. Faye bed-wet because she felt a tremendous lack of love. And then, as a psychological paradox, she was beaten for not feeling loved by the person who had caused her bed-wetting. This is hard. I know. Very hard. Between a stepfather and a regular father, there is no difference in a child's mind. He is the psychological father (which is much more important than being the biological father), and he hurt her deep in her soul. So through him, her first father figure, Faye Resnick learned to establish a negative relationship to men. Better father's spankings (for bed-wetting) than no relationship at all. Because a father figure who doesn't communicate at all is too strange. Better that he spanks.

And so Faye Resnick learned that men can't be trusted. Better to be careful from true emotions. And so all her life she would be one step ahead of everybody who could be useful to her......He, the stepfather, is responsible for the fact that Faye turned into a hardened person with an abnormal desire for admiration. It was her stepfather, the first prince, the first man, in Faye's life, who miserably failed and who drove her into addictions of all kind, be it drugs, alcohol or men. He turned her into just another Cinderella. Another woman who fled into alcohol and drugs.

Faye became just another aging Cinderella who couldn't point to more than $20,000 as the miserable leftover of a good life, when redecorating her home with Paul Resnick to the tune of $1.3 million, had been no big deal. My sources confirmed that Faye was in a panic! A panic that she might end up like her mother. Panic about who would pay her way in the future? Would Paul? Would Christian? Who would? The Starbucks boys didn't have money of their own. They expected Fayes to be rich and to pay for them. What if there wasn't any money left at all? What if she had to work? And where would she work? As a shop girl? In Beverly Hills, where everybody could see her? What if she would be kicked out then. Worse than when Camille kicked her out of the in disco, The Gate. And then—there will be more people like Camille who will kick her out!(**A12) (64) Depressions increased, so did the consumption of drugs and alcohol. Group therapy wasn't enough anymore. She panicked. And so, Ron's dream of a restaurant-cafe-thing was the exactly right thing that fit in Faye Resnick's plans. Because her personal desperation and fear for the future started the idea of a business venture with Nicole Simpson and Ron Goldman.

Faye Resnick became, in the final analysis , the driving force behind "Ron's restaurant thing" to get a grip on her life. She had no better idea than Ron's idea. She wanted to force her luck to help her make the impossible possible. To turn her life around and become "finally male independent" (her words) with a mere $20,000 in her pocket. The last pennies from a good life, and no prince in sight. But to turn her life around (and not be forced to change the lifestyle, to which she had grown accustomed) would have taken easily $500,000 cash on the table—if she intended to do serious business, something successful in one of the most expensive areas in the world. Or as the Browns call Ron's dream, the "restaurant thing." Or as Faye calls it, the "cafe."

As I said, I feel that nothing has been said in Faye's book without reason. Because it wasn't important to worry about making the book successful. Boring details about to whom it may concern just weren't important to the success of the book. Millions would doubtless have enjoyed getting an inside look at socialites who knew how to get rid of their frustrations by flirting with young men who were also looking for their big break. People would have been happy to read about sexual fantasies about "gorgeous young aspiring actors and good-looking guys who worked out," (66), the classic ambitious beach boys with "hard bodies," or, to read about how Nicole and Faye shared a lover, "so handsome, he looked hand-chiseled by the gods...the paramour of many well-to-do women in the Beverly Hills-Brentwood in-crowd." (67).

But again there is the same pattern repeated over and over again in this book. The unnatural thick ink spot, black and evil ink, in the middle of romantic tales of candlelight in bathrooms, and Nicole's sensuous initiation of sexual activity with Faye. (68) In the middle of tales about Nicole's strong sexual appetites, you read again about Faye Resnick's mortal terror—"I believe my life is in danger because of what I know." I believe that Faye does, in fact, fear death. I only doubt if she ever feared O.J. Simpson. What would she know about O.J. and Nicole's on and off relationship that was so life threatening? Because of all their friends and family—everybody knew what she knew. This was certainly not the reason for the murder of Ron Goldman and Nicole Simpson.

But she writes (To whom it may concern?), "As Nicole's best friend and O.J.'s confidante, I knew many devastating secrets. That is why I felt certain I was in danger!" (57) "But O.J. knows what I know. That's why I feel that I might be murdered." (62) She goes on, ".......it didn't matter how Nicole had died, I knew who had killed her, and now I was afraid I'd be killed for what I knew". (69) (I would like to clarify at this point that I am not repeating, again and again,, the same sentence from the same page in the book. These are Resnick's repetitions on different pages throughout the book.)

Here it is again! The triumph of knowing something the whole world is "dying" to know: "I knew who had killed her, and I was afraid I'd be killed for what I knew." She knew who had killed Nicole? Yes, I believe she knows indeed who killed Nicole, and that's why she does feel "a lot of guilt" for Ron Goldman, who had nothing to do with Nicole's and Faye's desperate attempt to become successful businesswomen who could invest half a million dollars in their enterprise

There is an old saying which reminds me of Faye Resnick: Every rumor contains some truth. And the rumors surrounding her full of drugs—and drug lords. Right? Yes, I know, everybody is skeptical when the subject of drug involvement comes up. Especially the subject of Colombian organized crime. But I'm not so sure what it is that makes so many people laugh, and cynically when the possibility of an execution murder is raised How much do they, who laugh and get cynical, know about drug people? Were they ever caught (perhaps accidentally) in the middle of such people's interest?

However, let me discuss drug people and their organization according to the drug people (i.e. members of organized crime). They are doubtlessly some of the most organized people (and enterprises) in the world. No doubt about it and at least TV movies have taught us to know that there isn't much room for jokes or laughter. They are cold, precise, silent, and they are everywhere. They have normal looking people who have infiltrated into places where we would never imagine. And someone who is in any way involved with them, would be crazy to overstep their boundaries. (On June 5th, 1995, sixty people were indicted in Miami because of their involvement with the "Colombian Drug Cartel," two prosecutors and one court official among them.)

"No, no," many people say. "The Colombian Mafia wouldn't kill this way." The truth is that the Colombian Mafia (which has been mentioned in the trial) has merged recently with the Russian and Italian Mafiosi. (70) Their firm regulations on how to kill might have changed, or perhaps this merger has modernized their methods, and perhaps sometimes they don't have time to think about following their own rules.

The Russian Mafia is, according to a CNN documentary, the "Fastest growing Mafia in the United States, now well-organized from the West Coast to the East." (70) It has become the biggest threat to, and is one of the biggest problems for, the United States. The Russians have their own ways and don't care what weapon (gun or knife) is used in their killings. The Colombians—it is true—practice the horrific custom of pulling the victim's tongue through their slit throat. But I believe they don't always have the time to carry out this ritual. And so from time to time, they do it the old-fashioned way, like the Italians do—with a gun, or sometimes a knife, or just a stick of dynamite in a chocolate box—depending on the circumstances.

In the course of the trial, serious people had begun to accept the idea of a conspiracy. CNBC's legal reporter, Manual Madrano, for example, has spoken of "a message by Colombian drug traffickers to acknowledge drug user Faye Resnick." (71) Meanwhile, the Colombian drug cartel's latest habit is to use their Russian partners for executions and killings. That means the professional killer comes from Russia to America, executes their job and leaves the U.S. the same or next day " back to Russia without leaving any trace." (72)

But let us examine what motive could have played the decisive role in the killing of Nicole Simpson (and Ron Goldman as perhaps the innocent bystander and dangerous eyewitness). Let's leave aside, for now, the theory that Nicole was unfortunately confused with the real target, Faye Resnick. Let us assume that this was, in fact, a typical (and pretty normal) drug retaliation murder. If so, the situation is very simple. First of all, the big bosses in the Colombian Mafia wouldn't care about "little fish" like Faye Resnick and Nicole Simpson. Let us assume that overdue payments, debts, or improper conduct as a dealer, played their part in this tragedy. Regardless of the amount of money and the criminal honor code— wrongdoing is wrongdoing and avenged.

Whatever its origin (Russian, Colombian, Italian) the Mafia acts like a corporation. There's a CEO, the big boss whose face almost nobody knows, (no photograph is allowed) and then there's the hierarchy stretching down to the smallest local authority. This local authority is responsible for a certain territory (for example Beverly Hills, or some other part of Los Angeles) and guarantees certain clients to certain dealers.

If a client fails to pay the local authority, or runs up a large debt, the local boss doesn't ask politely or beg for the money. He certainly can't sue and have his day in court. He just sets an example so that other clients won't cause him trouble. Because if the local authorities miscalculate their client's solvency or promise to pay, then they get in trouble with the bosses higher up, risking "punishment" themselves. This strict and brutal system (including its retaliations) is the only way the Mafia can function in our modern world. If they started to make exceptions and negotiate because some nice woman was involved, it would be the beginning of the end for the Mafia. Their best "little fish" are those who are addicted themselves (or greedy, or both) because these people will do anything the Mafia boss wants them to do. And if they fail, then they will be punished. Very simple. Everything clear-cut.

Faye Resnick is the person who was closest to Nicole Simpson during the last days of her life, and she was her closest friend. That means, she knew exactly what was going on. And why would she, the best friend, move out, if not for a reason?

Maybe Resnick could tell us why she moved out of her boyfriend's house into Nicole's house, and why she moved out of Nicole's house to another house in Beverly Hills, and then back and forth until she disappeared into a clinic . And why didn't she stay in her best friend's house in the end after all?

Would a person who knew something about such a brutal murder, speak right up? What about Resnick's boyfriend, who in my opinion should know a lot about what was going on? What about Nicole's other friends? They haven't come forward. On the contrary, they fight tooth and nail not to be involved. At no price. Like, for example, Christian Reichardt, Faye Resnick's fiancé at that time) and also my family members. (**A10) They all fear for their lives. Nobody wants to end up with their throats cut, ever so professionally, from one side to the other. Or as Johnny Cochran mentioned,"...where a good friend of hers [Faye] has been killed in another City in California...." (56) The only witnesses that are happy to talk are those whose lives are not in danger. People who, in front of the TV cameras, all of a sudden remember that they "noticed the dark looks, the evil eyes of O.J." But first, they want to make sure that their hair looks good, that their make-up is perfect, and that they are looking photogenic.

But Faye Resnick reveals more with the (subconscious) help of (her psychiatrist) Mike Walker than many witnesses would be able to do. With this pressure that she felt (by the way: before Nicole's death, and after Nicole's death—it didn't change), she needed someone who would listen. She needed to talk. And she talked, and talked, and talked. "Then came another horror," she says. "Word leaked to me via friends and reporters that O.J. and his lawyers had discussed floating the astounding and absolutely groundless claim that Nicole and I had borrowed money from Colombian drug dealers to open a Starbucks coffee shop, and that was why Nicole had been murdered! It's true that we'd been talking about putting up $35,000 (*A13) each to open a coffee house, but it was just talking....I sobbed to my lawyer, Arthur Barens. He suggested I make a tape in his office for the record, which I did, using the material from my diaries, before they were stolen. These tape recordings became the basis for this book." (73)

If this was such a "groundless claim" why was she "[sobbing] to her lawyer" (who then went to Istanbul for business.) (**A14) Why would she write that the defense planned to involve her with "Colombian drug dealers" and why would anyone need to argue in such great detail that opening a coffee house "was just talk"? If indeed, it was just talking. But the Browns in their book, also mention Ron's big dream, the "restaurant thing," so there was definitely more to it than just talk.

It is quite interesting what Faye tells us, "these tape recordings became the basis for this book." (73) Because she was also conveying the message: just in case you want to kill me, know that there are tapes in my lawyer's office. My life is in danger because of what I know. So be assured that I know enough to send you to prison. The timing wasn't an accident either. "Marcia, I just don't feel I can make a statement right now, although I certainly intend to do so. I will gladly appear for the prosecution as a character witness. But try to understand. I need time to collect myself and to calm down. I believe my life is in danger because of what I know." (52) And there is no doubt about what the witness for the prosecution would testify—about O.J.'s character and O.J.'s confiding in her. "As Nicole's best friend and O.J.'s confidante, I knew many devastating secrets. That is why I felt certain I was in danger!" Those to whom it is concerned, got the message.

"I felt a cold chill. 'Nicole,' I said shivering. 'I feel we're going to be killed. We have to go. Don't you see we're being set up?" Faye Resnick writes. (60) "I began to crumble under pressure. I couldn't take this constant feeling of doom. My chest felt constricted. I had to escape. I told Nicole, 'Please, let's just get out of here. Let's go to Europe. We can take our children, get a tutor. Or, you can take your kids to your mother's. And I'll take Francesca to Paul's house. The kids will be fine either way, but lets you and I get out of the country. We have the money, Nic. Let's go to St. Tropez, or to Mexico. Let's go anywhere. Let's just go." (74)

Such panic, such a constricted chest, such tremendous feelings of impending doom, and such pressure were supposed to be caused by of Othello's "if I can't have her, no one can"? Why would Faye Resnick, whose computer chip knows nothing but "Faye first," care about O.J. being violently angry? She knew how to dial 911—without any hesitation. Faye herself belittles 911 in her own words, "Poor 911" referring to the misuse of such an important emergency service by a woman like her, who start fights and then call 911 for amusement. (75)

And *why*—if O.J. was the reason for Resnick's cold chill and feelings of impending doom—why did *she* flee, instead of Nicole?

Immediately upon raising this question, I realized that we have again two very important stories written in only one sentence, to be contrasted with a dull, almost two-page story about Christian and some car keys. And of course, we don't read that Faye fled Nicole's house. But if we read between the lines, we can see that in Nicole's, Christian's and Kathy Harouche's house, a real drama must already have taken place: Faye's drama. Faye the puppeteer. The string puller. The one in whom Nicole genuinely believed. Faye, the role model for Nicole. Nicole wanted to be as tough as Faye. She wanted to be a woman who got her way. She didn't want to bite her fingernails anymore, or to run around like a Barbie doll. She wanted to be a tough businesswoman. One who could do something, do it on her own, without the first-class prince. "Nicole and I shared a dream. We wanted to stop being male-dependent..." writes Faye Resnick. "As long as I don't have to be dependent on any man. I'll have what I really want."

But such changes can't be forced. Not the way Faye thought they could be, the way she obviously told Nicole they should be. According to Faye's book, Nicole said, "Faye, the day you get out of here will be like our own independence day because O.J. is history. And I don't think you're too happy with Christian either." (76) As far as I remember, it was Nicole who wanted to marry O.J. He didn't force her. Did he?

Christian, too, has my sympathy, because as a chauffeur, he had always been good enough for Faye.

But perhaps she didn't like Christian anymore because he got fed up with Faye's doings and her drug problems. All this, for a decent chiropractor, was probably just too much. I would imagine that this was not the world he had dreamed of, to fear for his life. I rather assume that he wanted a woman who was his equal and could work together with him to build the biggest practice in Los Angeles. And how could he understand Faye's hysteria about O.J.? "What would O.J. want from her? He had fights with Nicole, not with Faye." And so Christian thought Faye Resnick was (in her own words) "paranoid," too. (77) "When I told him that O.J. had literally threatened over and over to kill Nicole, Christian said, 'You're overreacting. Guys say things like that all the time. He doesn't mean it.'" And Resnick writes further, "Christian and I continued to have problems at home. But I didn't want to confront him, I thought, leaving him might lift some of my pain. Deep in my soul, I felt something bad was coming."

Of course, this is true, that she knew something bad was coming. This was no longer "girlish" what was going on. This was dangerous. Life-threatening, dangerous! And what would Faye say to her friends about *why* she was panicking? She had to say something, at least. Anything, even to play Mrs. Stupid. So, O.J., the wife-beater, the batterer ("he didn't beat me for four years," said Nicole), the crazy Othello, who can't live without Desdemona—he was the reason for her fear.

Nobody believed her anyway, everybody thought she was hysterical. "Something bad was coming." (77) But they couldn't know that the fear was real. And the reason was real. Only the person was wrong. And since they all knew she was a little bit crazy and hysterical, why not let her make O.J. the target? Let her be crazy, who cares?

A couple of days before the gruesome murder, Faye Resnick "drove over to Nicole's, planning to stay there a while because Christian and I were having problems." (78) She then goes on to write about Nicole's story of O.J.'s threat. Normally, Faye takes herself very seriously. Here she should have written about their "having problems" in much more detail, painstakingly and tediously about every movement, why and how. But she doesn't.

Faye moved to Nicole's house, and the tragedy drew nearer and nearer. There is no doubt in my mind, Nicole knew exactly what was going on. She knew the problems. Severe problems. And she knew very well that Christian wasn't right this time. She knew that this time Faye wasn't paranoid. She knew that this time was indeed serious. But she trusted Faye completely and with all her heart. She must have believed that Faye, the strong, admired woman, would know how to deal with all their problems. But someone like Nicole, who had some luck (as Faye had not) and had leaped from daddy's castle into O.J.'s castle, just didn't understand what Faye Resnick's real world was all about. She certainly underestimated the situation. And anyway, she had to be loyal to her best friend, because they wanted together to be finally male-independent. So she wouldn't let her down, not Faye her best friend. That's part of the deal on "male independency." Perhaps she underestimated the danger she was in and perhaps believed (she must have believed) that she was innocent anyway. What would they do to her? Nothing.

She must have thought, "If they're out to punish Faye, then Faye should leave, get herself to a safe place! And if they come, I'll tell them she's gone, and that she's doing everything to solve the problem." But perhaps Nicole was much more (unwanted) involved, and didn't know it. Not really. We don't know what Faye told her, and we don't know whether she made up stories or not. The fact is that Nicole remained in her house. If she had known what was coming, she would have done as Faye Resnick did. She would have fled.

"I felt a cold chill.....I feel we're going to be killed. We have to go. Don't you see, we're being set up?" says Faye Resnick. And she's telling the truth. I can feel it. And that the illogic is perfect because O.J. wanted to kill Nicole, Faye fled to Kathy Harouche's house? "It was up on Mulholland Drive, a gated community called Beverly Park, the most exclusive section of Beverly Hills. When the guards opened the massive gates, I drove through and literally breathed a heavy sigh of relief. As the gates closed behind me, I finally felt safe." (79) All this excitement, cold chills, fear of being "set up ," saying she "literally breathed a heavy sigh of relief... [and] as the gates closed behind me, I finally felt safe." All of this just because O.J. Simpson is running around like King Kong with a big knife in his hand, with crazed eyes, screaming, "Where is Faye, where is Faye! I wanna kill her! I wanna kill her!"

No, like it or not, if Othello, the murderer of passion, obsession, and rage, had killed Nicole (and Ron out of jealousy) then Faye would never ever have had, like Lyle Menendez, the feeling that her "chest was constricted." She wouldn't have "crumble[d] under the pressure." She certainly wouldn't have had "this constant feeling of doom." And above all, she wouldn't have been troubled by a guilty conscience! She wouldn't be saying things like, "I feel a lot of guilt. I don't know why, and I know it's irrational. Nothing I did caused Ron's murder. But it's just something that will bother me forever."

But again, Faye Resnick uses the right words for that what really happened. She speaks herself of being set up. "Don't you see we're being set up?" she says. And she's telling the truth. But would Othello set up Desdemona? How could anyone set up anyone in a rage of jealousy? It is just impossible. Because a rage is a rage. And a setup is a setup. But this "setup" is, in my opinion, the reason for Faye Resnick's guilty conscience toward Ron Goldman (and not toward Nicole Simpson, because, Nicole, I believe, knew what was going on). Because only Ron did *not* know that his dream of a restaurant was trapped in a deadly triangle.

O.J., according to what he put in writing, must suffer tremendously about not having continued to protect Nicole as he did for seventeen years, because he knew that she was in trouble because of Faye. Today, he knows that he could have saved her life, but he didn't. He was childish and was busy annoying her with the IRS. He knows that it was a fault to clear off the field for Faye Resnick and have her use Nicole for her own goals. And this hurts tremendously. And certainly for the rest of his life. He will always live with the feeling that it was his fault, that he didn't protect Nicole as he could have done. "As I've said, I have been totally unjudgmental people [person] all my life. It's a fault of mine. I now find it a fault. I know in my heart that the answer to the death of Nicole and Mr. Goldman lies somewhere in the world that Faye Resnick inhabited." (80)

Can you see for yourself the difference—O.J. speaks of *fault*, and Faye Resnick speaks of *guilt*! I will discuss later in this book, O.J.'s "fault" in more detail, but wanted to demonstrate at this point the psychologically important difference between fault or admitting one's guilt, and thus involvement.

"...I faced the fact that my dearest friend, [Nicole], who had tried so hard to save my life, had lost her own," writes Faye Resnick. (69) There it is again! The overwhelming and irresistible mixed feelings of guilty conscience and triumph that culminate in self-accusation.

Nicole "tried so hard" to save Faye's life, and "had lost her own"—what does Faye (subconsciously and thus really) mean by such statements? She tells us exactly what she says: that Nicole tried hard to save

Faye's life. And as we know, Nicole did send Faye to Kathy Harouche in Beverly Hills, where she "literally breathed a heavy sigh of relief. As the gates closed behind me [Faye], I finally felt safe." And so Nicole "had lost her own [life]." This is what Faye Resnick is telling the world.

What reason would Nicole have had at this time, in June 1994, to kick Faye Resnick out of her house? And if she didn't kick her out, what reason would Faye have had to move into Kathy's house, instead of staying with their best friend, Nicole? Or what reason would Faye have had to go from Christian to Nicole, from Nicole to Kathy, from Kathy to Christian, and from there to the clinic?

The trap of The Deadly Triangle was closing in on her. One side of the triangle has already been laid to rest in two cold coffins. One side of the triangle will be silent as a grave. And one side of the triangle will be silenced because he is Othello, and Othello is guilty by nature. "Girl I need to talk to you." O.J. tried desperately to speak with Faye at the funeral. (81) And in this light Faye's description of O.J. looking "zombie-like, speaking in a raspy, strained voice, that sounded like it came from some private hell" becomes clear. How else would he look or sound? Because despite their chaotic relationship, he loved Nicole. She was his baby, whom he had laid to rest.

Here it is again in Faye Resnick's own words! "How did we let this happen to you?" is her comment at the funeral, (82) looking into the grave—perhaps shivering and thinking, "It could have been me!" Yes, I can imagine that this was in Faye Resnick's mind. And again her guilty conscience, stemming from her religious background, allowed her to speak (at least via her psychiatrist, Mike Walker, and through the medium of the written statement, the book): How did we "let this happen" to you?

Yes, I believe that Faye Resnick was "terrified" by O.J. on the day of the funeral. I believe her when she says that something must have "constricted her chest" and it was certainly not an easy task to look into O.J.'s eyes, behind which she knew was an intelligent man who "knows what she knows." She probably thought to herself, "That's why I feel that I might be murdered." (62) Hounded and tortured by mortal terror, Faye appeared at Nicole's funeral, knowing that it could happen again at any moment and this time to her. This mortal terror strengthens the need to convey a plot, which normally would have been impossible in such a strong emotional situation. If the feelings are true in a situation like this everyone is normally hugging everyone else. Of course, with such chilling feelings, knowing that she could be the one lying in the coffin, the voice became so "strong" that Faye could only say, "It surprised me."

Why was she surprised? I don't know. Everybody in her place would have done the same, would have had just one thought in their mind: to survive. And after I read her book, I felt that this was for Faye Resnick a question of life or death, of prison or freedom. "O.J. this is not the time. This is about

Nicole," and she pulled her hands away and went straight to Justin and Sydney. (81) If we were to ask O.J. Simpson why he said, "Girl, I need to talk to you." Would we believe him? No, we wouldn't. And Faye knows this now, too. She knows that she has nothing to fear from him. And she knows that meanwhile, O.J.'s statements like, "It was all her fault, Mom" [Nicole's fault]—nobody wants to understand. Because whatever O.J. says in his defense, just "Doesn't make sense," as Mike Walker said about this statement. (83)

But at the funeral, it couldn't be otherwise. O.J. knew at this very moment that the only person who knew everything, was Nicole's girlfriend, the confidante who lived with her the last days. She knew everything, like every best girlfriend in this world. Who else would know better than Faye? She knew what was going on the last days, and why she moved in and out. And he knew that she was probably the only witness to the murder.....

I believe that O.J. knew that Faye knew whether it was just a case of mistaken identity, or whether Nicole was already so much involved in a certain naive way in Faye's drug chaos, but seeing only the "male independency" and not the great danger she was in. Because if all this weren't the case, then her own words, "I feel a lot of guilt" and "Nothing I did cause [sic] Ron's murder," just wouldn't have been there. I believe that it's true—this will bother her forever.

But there are still many other questions that bother me: Why is Denise Brown denying her boyfriend is the Mafioso Tony "The Animal" Fiato? (84) Why would anybody suddenly make their will at a young age, like Nicole at thirty-five? Why would the editor of *The Star*, Mr. Frost, state that Kato would know who the murderers were and that it all has something to do with drugs? Why would the Brown family and Faye Resnick point exclusively to O.J. as the only murderer and yet they all don't speak to each other? Faye Resnick doesn't talk to Kato. Denise doesn't talk to Kato. Kato doesn't talk to Juditha. Why all this animosity?

"Nicole's the one who's not here to defend herself against those lies," inveighs O.J. and furthermore, he says, "What annoys me about Faye is that Faye has done this to Nicole. Not me!" (85) He is right, Nicole cannot speak anymore. She can't tell us her side of the story, like for example about lesbian encounters with Faye Resnick, that perhaps never took place. She must accept that Faye portrays herself as an innocent woman who "would never ever have initiated a physical relationship with a woman. Never in a million years." (86) But has then, surprisingly, been seduced by an allegedly oversexed Nicole! (As if somebody like Faye Resnick were unable to resist such unwanted approaches.) Even if this were true, and the lesbian love scene, as told by Faye Resnick, had taken place, a real best friend would keep such things silent and the memory of the dead "best friend" , and for the rest of one's life, holy.

"I know in my heart that the answer to the death of Nicole and Mr. Goldman, lies somewhere in the world that Faye Resnick inhabited," writes O.J. Simpson in his written statement, his book. While I was looking for O.J.'s self-accusation, I found his comment about his ex-wife and him being "at peace with each other" but, "once again Faye Resnick interfered [with] our relationship." But perhaps this psychological phenomenon, the compulsive self-accusation could be the only chance for Nicole to defend herself from her chilly grave and perhaps to take revenge for that what has been done to her.

In my opinion as a professional person with years of research and experience behind me, I am convinced that Faye Resnick knows a lot more than she is telling us—and was probably the only witness to the murder. Mr. Gil Garcetti stated on October 8th "...If they brought any evidence he would re-open the case ." Yes, he should seriously consider this step.

But as I will explain later in the chapter, "The Race Card," self-confidence is a very deep thing.

CHAPTER FOUR
The Race Card

On Tuesday, June 14, twenty-four-hours after the bodies of Nicole Brown Simpson and Ronald Goldman were found in the courtyard of Nicole's condominium at 875 South Bundy Drive, O.J. Simpson walked upstairs into his master bedroom suite at 360 North Rockingam Avenue. (87) O.J.'s sisters, Shirley and Carmelita, their children and grandchildren, were worried about their mother, Eunice Simpson's, health. O.J. was exhausted. Between landing in Chicago at 4:15 a.m. and being summoned by police at 5:45 a.m. and told to fly back to Los Angeles, he had gotten little sleep. After his flight had landed, O.J. had been driven by limousine to his house, been handcuffed, and taken to police headquarters, where he had allowed himself to be questioned for over three hours without his attorney, Howard Weitzman (who tried to physically stop O.J.!), present, which was later interpreted as the ultimate admission of his guilt.

O.J. had spent much of the time since coming home from the police station on one of two facing couches in his den, wearing the same white golf shirt and black pants he had put on in his Chicago hotel room that morning. Mostly, he was flanked by two men who, after Al Cowlings and football star Marcus Allen, were closest to him. (88) The TV sets showed Nicole's and Ron's sheeted bodies being carried through the courtyard's thick foliage; there was O.J. in handcuffs, talking to Detective Phil Vannatter; and there was O.J. strolling, solemn, head down, into police headquarters. Every report implied that he was the only suspect. The re-reporting of his 1989 New Year's Day beating of Nicole, stirred up the viewer. Four heavy conflicts in seventeen years turned him into a psychopath, called wife-beater and last but not least, into Othello— "If I can't have her, nobody can." "Can you believe this? Can you believe what they're saying about me?" O.J. called out. "They're making a bigger deal out of this than it was!" (89)

And so the audience of this fact-based soap opera, changed from thirty percent guilty to eighty-five percent guilty and not even Dr. Henry Lee's bombshell testimony about unidentified shoeprints, fingerprints on paper, not collected pieces of paper, or the two killer theory, as well as Mark Fuhrman's loss of credibility, was able to change people's minds fundamentally. Despite all efforts of the dream team and despite the juror's explanation that they felt they had to obey the law (which means, the prosecution hasn't proven their case beyond a reasonable doubt) fifty-six percent disagree with the verdict, and only thirty-three percent agree. They are convinced that O.J. is guilty as hell and got away with murder. Yes, there is no doubt, the majority believe O.J.was the only murderer (or at least part of the "two killer theory").

Many with whom I discussed argued, "No, no, O.J. is guilty! He wanted to flee the country. This convinced me of his guilt. If he were innocent, he would have gone to the police. Right away! He wouldn't have staged such a circus. He wouldn't have taken his passport, A.C., and $10,000 dollars. And a ride in a white Bronco wouldn't have turned into one of the most famous car trips ever. It's true, many wouldn't have reacted as O.J. did. They would have known that people would immediately interpret this as an admission of guilt.

But I argued, that possibly many others would have reacted the same way as O.J. did . He reacted hysterically, childishly and he panicked. He couldn't handle the stress. His 100 billion neurons in his brain were turned upside down. As he said himself later in the interview with the police, he was "weird." Yes, if he didn't do, he must indeed have been totally weird, perhaps even on the verge of a nervous breakdown. The only princess of his life (regardless of the on and offs) had been brutally murdered. And (if he didn't do it) he hadn't even had a chance to mourn her death before he was trapped, in danger of being murdered, too—psychologically.

O.J. repressed "his blackness" all those years (according to the Brown family.) But in reality, it was not the blackness that he repressed, but his fear of the image that has been developed of being black. "I grew up black. I grew up in a ghetto. It isn't like I wasn't aware of racism. I just chose not to let it define my life. I chose not to let it control me," says O.J. Simpson. (90) But O.J. at that very moment, accused of being one of the cruelest murderers of our century and under such stress, forgot all his good intentions to ignore social problems. He couldn't think rationally anymore. He couldn't remember that we have a legal system to protect him, that lawyers would fight for his rights. His billions of neurons told him something else—they will find you guilty! One way or another. The only thing he was aware of was that he was "weird," because he was totally under stress. And under stress, our brains do very strange things. Call it blacking out, flipping out, whatever. We know this happens.

But with Al Cowlings, he could have a blackout or a nervous breakdown after the cruel and tragic murder of Nicole. With A.C., he could even react like a little boy. With A.C., he could be childish, he could take the passport and the money—and could play "Punch in our Punch and Judy show." He could even put a pistol to his head and call hysterically for his mom so he could see her for the last time in his life. His mom, who again should be strong and perhaps would be the only one who knew a way out. His mom, who always knew that the glass of beer was still half full.

And so, a desperate man, not ready to be accused of the Murder of the Century—this man was nearly out of his mind and certainly didn't know how to handle the stress. He hoped that all his father figures — Al Cowlings, Howard Weitzman, Robert Kardashian, and Robert Shapiro —would have the solution and a way out of this drama. But they didn't. And they couldn't, because O.J. had already been chosen to be Othello, the jealous Moor who killed his white wife.

O.J., who had repressed social problems from an early age, was not prepared for what would come. In his mind, the classical lynching of a black man, symbolized by the "N-word," was about to take place. I can imagine that pictures of hanging men on trees, burned Christian crosses, and bold-headed Neo-Nazis flashed through O.J.'s mind. Nicole was white—he is black! For O.J., it was the end, regardless of whether he was guilty or completely innocent. "So it's like white America says a white woman shouldn't go out with a black guy, and blacks say you shouldn't go out with a white woman," he says. And how could his 100 billion neurons come to any other conclusion then, they would hang him no matter what?

Naked fear overwhelmed his rational thinking. Forgotten stories from his ghetto childhood awakes, "When I was age seven or eight, I was going by train with my family to Louisiana to visit relatives. When we got to Dallas, they made us pull the curtains [down] all around our compartment in the railroad car we were riding in. Not all of us blacks were in one car—it was supposed to be an integrated car until we got to Texas!" (91) I wouldn't be surprised that he started to count his "white blood drops," which was supposed to make him better in the eyes of the detectives and of course, less guilty. "My mother has Native American blood on her side, and on my father's side, there is southern white blood. Sometime back, my great-grandmother was taken advantage of by some plantation owner. My great-grandmother's family raised the baby, the white man couldn't be exposed," O.J. explains. And he goes on, "Despite some mixed blood here and there, as a kind, I looked at myself as just being black." (92) And he tells the experiences he had with racists South

Africans, who consider themselves (because of "white blood") "superior to blacks, and...were thought to have a higher status than people of pure African background." (93) I don't want to comment on such superior maniacs at this point, but I will discuss later in this book the "white, blue, or black blood" mirage—and especially what racism is all about! First, I will discuss the regular red blood that we all have in our veins.

O.J.'s red blood was in commotion. To be black and to be a suspect in a murder case, there wasn't a repression mechanism that could have been strong enough to repress his fear of the police. An ill-famed authority with a long history and record of injustice against the black man. If we want to understand some of O.J.'s actions and reactions, then we have to try to see his point, the mortal fear of authorities. Regardless of how primitive and intellectually inferior police officers sometimes are, they have (with their police badge) at this very moment the absolute power. And although there shouldn't be any human being in the 1990s who would have such kind of power, there are still enough police departments around the country whose record shows police injustice toward black men, right?

O.J.'s first lesson on how to behave like a black man toward police and to be docile, happened at a very young age: "I learned real quick that you have to become as docile as possible with the police. This was my first lesson on becoming docile around the police.......These two police officers put us up against the wall...... I became real docile again." (94) Other incidents (from twenty years back) awake like a flash, and he remembers Peter Fonda's ("he was all for causes") taking him into a "white only" restroom at the airport in South Africa. "It was strange walking into this toilet with a cutout of a black figure above the door with a red line through it. It was like being in the South in the fifties." (92). Or another story, "I was stopped in Beverly Hills with Nicole. The cop claimed I had run a light. I hadn't, but I knew if I argued with him, he probably would have ticketed me. I felt vulnerable. So once again, I just became docile." (94)

O.J.'s subconscious confession tells us why he reacted illogically, yes, even stupidly. "I've always known about racism. It's when any race feels superior over another race......Two years ago, if somebody wrote me a racist letter, my assistant, Cathy, would not have even shown it to me. I dealt with the issue by ignoring it...I ignored racism. Since I was a kid, I've avoided negatives. I always insulated myself from the subject of skin color." (96) But this time he wasn't accompanied by his colleague Peter Fonda, and he wasn't only a co-starring actor in a movie called *Diamond Mercenaries*, this time the nightmare of every African American male had come true: he was the suspect in a double homicide case, he was under the authority of the ill-famed LAPD—he was at the mercy of a race that feels superior over dark skin.

But he is, almost thirty years later, again docile and went voluntarily to the LAPD to answer the detective's questions. I am sure he believed in his naive way, that it was the right move to talk to the authorities (whom he had feared his entire life), to tell them about his complete innocence, charm them (as he normally would). I can imagine that he believed that no blot on his record would remain and believed, that the matter would be over as soon as he had answered all the detective's questions and that it would be sufficient to be again "docile around the police." Perhaps he thought that the whole world, and the detectives, would believe in his innocence.

But the detectives Philip Vannatter and Tom Lange would look at him with their cold eyes. Merciless. Eyes that made me even shiver. Eyes that I believe must have made O.J. feel that he is already condemned. And he was condemned, at least by Detective Philip Vannatter, Tom Lange, and Marc Fuhrman. He was already chosen by them to be the raging Othello who killed his wife. (**A16) And not only by them but also by eighty percent of all Americans, because almost everybody judges O.J.'s interrogation tapes, recorded twenty-four hours after the murder, to be the ultimate admission of his guilt. Comments like Geraldo Rivera's became common. "The tone of the voice is mysterious." But on the other hand, there were also people like Vincent Balliosi, who has stated on *Hard Copy*, "If O.J. were guilty, he wouldn't have subjected himself to being grilled by the LAPD." (97)

As we know from the tapes, O.J. giggles nervously, tries to charm the officers, and tells them a lot of nonsense, hoping to win the understanding of his interlocutors (Detectives Philip Vannatter and Detective

Tom Lange), believing (and hoping) that they are talking "man to man," that they, too, might have had marital problems, and that they might have some sympathy for a man who feels himself mentally battered. I know from many cases with men involved who feel in similar situations like an unjustly treated child.

I am sure that O.J. felt the same way and tried to communicate this to Vannatter and Lange, and tried to get their sympathy by saying things like, "they [the police] never took my statement, they never wanted to hear my side, they never wanted to hear the housekeeper's side." (**A17)

I can imagine that O.J. hoped that the men across from him would be able to identify with a so-called "macho man" who had been pretty much finished by his own princess. "Hey, she hit me. Nicole was drunk, she did her thing." He tries to explain. "And I—didn't punch her. No, I wrestled her is all I did." According to his reactions on tape, he was in deadly fear, that people will deduce from such marriage problems that he actually committed such a terrible act. "But I—I—I—you know...." I can imagine that he hopes the man across from him will understand. But the questioner doesn't beat his wife. His wife doesn't take drugs and most certainly doesn't drink. He's not even divorced. His wife certainly wouldn't make troubles and attack him. And I'm sure that his wife wouldn't have given her lover the red Ferrari. How could he understand?

"Nicole is a strong girl," says O.J. trying to justify their marriage problems and their physical fights. "She's a—one of the most conditioned women—since that period of time she's hit me a few times...." "Nicole was drunk when she did her thing." Yes, she did her thing, but how could Detective Vannatter and Detective Lange know what her thing was? They just knew that O.J. was Othello, and the only suspected murderer in the high-profile case they had been waiting for!

And so several hours after the murder of his wife, he made the most ridiculous statement in an interrogation that anyone in such a situation could have made. O.J. was consumed by stress and naiveté. This terrible stress that keeps us sweating, stuttering, trembling, shivering, fainting, making mistakes and being "weird." O.J. knew that he was "the number one target ," yes, this he knew. "And now you're telling me I got blood all over my place." Yes, he heard what the detectives said, but I can imagine that he didn't understand the full implication. "But I never touched her after that," says O.J. in his defense and means by that the four years pause not having conflicts. And it must be true, as I said, I heard the tapes with Nicole herself (giggling and flirtatious) saying that they hadn't had any physical fight for four years. (98) "I loved her, I didn't want us to separate...." Vincent Bolliosi stated, "If he were guilty he would not admit that the breaking up was his part." (97)(**A18)

When Detective Lange asked, "What do you think happened? Do you have any idea?" O.J. reacted almost as he would have under normal circumstances. His voice sounded angry—He raised his voice. "I have no idea, man, I......".

Someone, who believed in the concept of being "docile" with police and who was guilty would remain calm and patient—which O.J. certainly was not. He almost lost his temper, but made an effort to calm down. "But you guys haven't told me anything! Every time I ask, you guys say you're going to tell me in a bit. I—I have no idea what happened. When you have said to my daughter, [Arnelle] said something to me today that somebody else might have been involved. I had absolutely no idea what—what happened, I don't know how, why, or what!"

Racist or not, character or not, temptation or not, planted glove or not, planted blood or not—certainly most LAPD detectives involved in this case couldn't think anything except "O.J. is the only possible murderer," especially when they found drops of blood like the trails of Hansel and Gretel. The "marriage syndrome" sure helped, though, for any other conclusion. Obviously, not one of those detectives would have thought, just for a second, that perhaps those trails are a little bit too Hansel and Gretel-like, too obvious. The evidence is a bit too striking and some details a bit too accurate.

And by the way, according to the prosecution's theory, O.J. must have been dripping blood non-stop from 10:15 to 10:45. This would mean, according to experts, O.J. was bleeding for thirty-five minutes, which means, that there should have been at least 200 drops of blood in the Bronco. "Unless somebody has blood problems or is taking medication, like aspirin, he would bleed for five to eight, at the maximum, ten minutes."

But why should they have thought this? They are no lawyers, no politicians, no Washington's spin doctors, no DNA experts, no coroners, no lab experts, no forensic experts, no Nobel prize winners—and they are not the District Attorney. They just deliver what they see and what they believe in. And this was blood, drip-drip-drip, and a bloody glove in the house of a man they had known for years as a superstar from TV, driving by with expensive cars, not even looking at them or saying hello, parking his car in a casual manner (which they later will interpret as being very unusual), and having marriage problems with his wife.

My husband is a very technologically and rationally-oriented person. Blood had convinced my husband that O.J. was guilty—and blood has changed his mind. See for yourself his logical theory, which has been confirmed by many physicians. He said, "According to the prosecution's case, O.J., after having committed the murders at Nicole's house, ran out of the back gate and left eight to ten drops of blood behind. He left the door open so his children would see the grizzly murder of their mother and her friend. He ran to his car, smeared a drop of blood on the Bronco's body, smeared some blood inside, and must have driven around the area for fifteen minutes, looking for a place to hide the knife and the bloody clothes (in a place that he had supposedly chosen long before the killing). Then O.J. drove home and arrived roughly 10:40 p.m. according to the limo driver's testimony and walked quietly outside the fence, threw the glove into his estate, behind Kato Kaelin's quarters, returned to his car, walked from his car to his house leaving behind him (drip-drip-drip) nine to ten drops of blood again, and entered the house leaving one drop of blood in the foyer." And no other drops of blood have been seen anywhere else. O.J. is supposed to have lost all that blood in Nicole's house, and in the Bronco, there's only a small smear. But in that Bronco, if he hadn't stopped bleeding, there should have been at least 150 or 200 drops. According to the evidence at the crime scene, he lost 10 drops of blood in a minute. And there is not a drop between the foyer and the bedroom. Nothing was found along the fence, on the wall, or even beside the glove. And why didn't the limo driver see any injury? And the stewardesses who served O.J. during his flight to Chicago? And why didn't the dog discover the trail of blood immediately (as every dog does), and why didn't the limo driver destroy any of the blood drops, but left them neatly spaced, one by one, from the gate to the house ?

And it was "their O.J." when the officers were called from time to time via 911 by Nicole Simpson. The detectives did what they believed was right and what would solve the case so that they, would be known for the rest of their lives as "those cops who booked O.J. Simpson."

However, during the trial, it happened that more and more rumors flew and evidence hardened, that there is much more to this case than just a behavior-disturbed man, who obviously hates his mother in every woman. They came up with questions like, "Did Marc Fuhrman plant the glove?" He was the first who jumped over the wall without a search warrant and went alone, without a backup officer behind O.J.'s estate and found the bloody glove. (By the way, I don't buy the common explanation, that, because he didn't wear a jacket, he couldn't have carried a glove. Of course, he could: in his trousers.) And what is the matter with Philipp Vannatter? Vannatter, who worked, according to Professor Stan Goldman, on 5,500 cases and never held the blood of a suspect for some hours, "but just with O.J.'s blood he was driving around twenty-one miles and holding on to it there for some hours." (99) And Judge Ito's statement about Vannatter's "reckless disregard for the truth" might enter into history.

Is this perhaps the Conspiracy of the Century? Could it mean that our police officers and prosecutors are criminals themselves, involved in the greatest conspiracy of all time? Remember, sixty people were indicted in June 1995 in Miami, because of their involvement with the "Colombian Drug Cartel," - among them two prosecutors and court officials. If this is so, then valuable trails, traces, and evidence must have been destroyed. And the authorities believe they have caught the only murderer—while the murderer could still be out. The murderer could be sitting every day and every night watching TV, (even the aftermath) perhaps the one whose blood Nicole had under her fingernails. But why are we talking about "police conspiracy" if there are perhaps only one or two black sheep who made a boo-boo? Mark Fuhrman brags about manufacturing evidence of suspects with the screenwriter Laura McKinney, and of course he shows off about himself and his group's pseudo-strength. "They knew damn well I did it, but there was nothing they could do about it. We were tight, I mean, we could have murdered people. We all knew what to say." (100) (**A19)(**A20)

But how far a racist with his abnormal desire for admiration can go, is demonstrated by Mark Fuhrman's confession, "I am the key prosecution witness in the Trial of the Century. If I go down, and the glove goes out, their case goes bye-bye." (100) (Again, compared in a later chapter with Faye Resnick's, Lyle Menendez and Timothy McVeigh's compulsive behavior: what would be a heroic deed without an audience?) Interestingly enough—,Marc Fuhrman, Lyle Menendez and Faye Resnick, all needed psychiatric help.

Be that as it may, let us take what Dr. Wecht has said, namely that Philip Vannatter made, in fact, (who learned how to play together as a team) a boo-boo and that Marc Fuhrman is playing, against his will, a part in this soap opera by doing a big favor for the professionals who have a strong interest in diverting attention from their involvement, by pointing to O.J. as the only murderer. There is no doubt, it's part of underworld business to be familiar with the racist mentality of some police officers. They could be sure that some police officers with the Othello Syndrome in their mind, would complete their mission.

We are, unfortunately, fixed on two conclusions—either O.J. is Othello or Fuhrman is a racist in charge of a great police conspiracy and are excluding other possibilities, of which, at least, the "police sloppiness" became an established reality. "Spreading the blanket over one of the bodies could have brought with it hair or fibers," explains Dr. Wecht, and the same can happen with blood, "a physical transfer." On the other hand, DNA science is dependent on accuracy, proper collection of blood, and proper storage. And then DNA science is simply too young to have absolute sure results, or there is even the problem, "No two people have the same DNA, but two people can have the same test result." (104) I believe, that almost everybody knows in the meantime about the missing blood, Vannatters driving twenty-one miles with a little tube of O.J.'s blood, no security at the lab, uncounted blood swatches, Ron Goldman's shirt being improperly stored, unidentified fingerprints of "nine people ," and unidentified blood under Nicole's fingernails, etc.

It's only logical that a lot of traces must have been destroyed, (instead of preserved) because the detectives were fixed on the idea that they have caught the long-awaited and only possible murderer, Othello, who couldn't be otherwise than obsessed with his ex-wife. (Obsessed as, for example, a man like Mark Fuhrman and his psychological problems would be with a woman like Nicole Simpson.)

"Mark Fuhrman is the star-witness of the Government," says the attorney Barry Scheck. But on the other hand, it is established that, "psychiatric reports confirm that he is a racist." (105) And the psychiatric report is supported by tapes. Heavy tapes that are meant to be the basis for a movie. Regardless whether he is inventing characters for a film script, it is always his emotions, his hate, his love, his envy. For this reason, the screenwriter, Laura McKinney wanted him as the "real-life source." Fact-based stories are bestselling stories. Laura McKinney knows that, or course. And so, one can hear hours of insult, discrimination, hate—tapes that are just vulgar and cheap polemic, since it is every racist's language in this world. Because this language *is* the reason why they are called racists. If they are alone, they usually don't act out/execute their verbal threats . For this, they need the group. So called "racists" need the group badly. They need the strength of the group and the unifying target of hate. Here they have at least the feeling of strength. Or in Mark Fuhrman words, "We were tight....we all knew what to say." The group, the holding together of the group, this is the basis and reason for men to decide to become a racist.

But what is a racist? Or better I should ask, what do we believe why people are becoming "racists ?" We believe and accept without any criticism that it is legitimate for some people to hate the Jews, Blacks, Hispanics, homosexuals, foreigners and of course, women. We do not even think about that neither the Jews, nor the women, neither Hispanics, homosexuals or foreigners are anything but, a "different race"! At least, not as long as we believe that "racism" would have something to do with "race" and furthermore, if we accept that religion, gender, sexual orientation and skin color create different races among the human race. But this is not the case.

The word "race" comes from the field of biology and refers to "geographically distinct groups within a plant and animal species if individuals with modifications are designated." (106) Originally we all were brown. All human beings, regardless of whether their pigmentation activity continues to function or has degenerated, belong to the familia of Hominidae, the genus of Homo, the species of Homo sapiens, the order of primates, the phylum of Chordata, and the class of Mammalia—because we all can walk upright, all have a developed brain and chin. all can learn the same things, and all belong to the subspecies of Homo sapiens . Since we all belong to the same familia, the same genus, the same species, the same order, the same phylum, the same class, and we all have pigmentation granules in our skin, we all belong, seen in strictly biological terms, to the same race, namely, the human race.

To be a Jew is not a race but to belong to the Jewish faith. If, for example, a Tom Metzger would make statements that he hates Jews, meaning, he hates people of a special religion. No more and no less. The concept of an Aryan is Adolf Hitler's personal invention due to his neurosis and personal tragic, and repressed desire, for symbiosis with the Jews themselves. Adolf, plainly put, wanted just to be like those whom he hated from childhood on and his entire life: he wanted to be a Jew. He wanted to have the same image of being smart, powerful and wealthy. And if possible, also famous. He wanted to be like his grandfather. But his grandfather rejected him, the little Adolf. So how can somebody want to be bad like somebody whom he hates on the other hand? This conflict, this emotional distress, this ended up in the repressed desire for symbiosis! Mixed with his envy and pathological inferiority complex, his insecurity in school (and envy of Jewish classmates) and the lacking Identification Phase with his Mother resulted in one of the biggest frenzies in history.

The paradox itself is demonstrated by Adolf Hitler's choosing just all the Jews to be the outlet to divert from his self-hatred. But as I said, the neurosis has been bred by Adolf's father, himself, and is connected to Adolf's own Jewish grandfather. Adolf's father, Alois, couldn't handle the reality of the nineteenth century, to be the "illegitimate baby" of his mother Anna Maria Schicklgruber, who had a child together with the wealthy Austrian Jew, Mr. Frankenberger. This child, Alois, was Adolf Hitler's father. Alois was obviously never able to overcome this psychological problem of inferiority, and so Adolf Hitler's father, Alois Schicklgruber, forged forty years later the entry in the old registry book from June 7, 1837 and went from then on (January 1877), by the name of Alois Hitler. (107) Fundamentally, Adolf lived in fear of exposure.

Of his true origins, which were in such flagrant contradiction of the legend he created. Joachim C. Fest explains, "He bragged to all his classmates that he came from a good family." (107)   (*A21 and **A22) Even as the Fuehrer of the rising Nazi Party (NSDAP), he reacted hysterically and found it "insulting" if anyone dared to ask him about his family or the circumstances of his life. Adolf wanted to be "nobody's son," as he said. (108) He obscured, disguised and altered his family origins and unhappy existence as a tramp, thief, and beggar.

The whole Aryan idea is nothing more than a mirage of a sad little boy, who was poor and desperate and as Hitler's biographer Joachim C. Fest explains, "did not have a bedstead anymore, but instead had to sleep in a cattle trough" (110). A desperate boy. who dreamed of god Wotan and [goddess] Valhalla, who would free him from this sort of life and would make him powerful. I have no doubt that Adolf couldn't agree more with the Austrian, Frido von Liszt's, who was the first racist who had "visions of Wotan." It is interestingly enough, (and to understand Adolf's culmination of his psychological problems) that Austria itself, famous for its anti-Semitic attitude, "saw (as collective societal identity problems) their identity in Germany." (111) Thanks to the circumstances of that time the Austrian, Adolf Hitler, found indeed enough like-minded, downtrodden people, who loved him for having given them finally an identity (and miracle medicine) and to be somebody they never dreamed of, an Aryan!

Color (the other corpus delicti for justifying racism) is a chemical reaction of the pigmentation granules that exist in all human beings as the protective mechanism of nature designed to protect internal organs, skin, eyes, and hair against ultraviolet solar radiation. (**A24) People who don't have this protective pigmentation are very ill and are called Albino. Due to a pathological disorder in his largest organ, the skin, he has no pigmentation at all. This gave him not only snow-white hair but also pink eyes. His skin and eyes are abnormally sensitive to light, and his vision is often impaired. He is oversensitive because his internal organs are not protected, either. (***A23) I don't believe that any "racist" would like to live the life of an Albino—just to be an "Aryan," which then, would be, in fact, "pure white." About Hispanics, there is not much to say, except that they are neither pure Spaniards or mixed with Aztecs, Incas, and Mayas. So, how could anyone justify racism about Hispanics? They are like everybody of our large family, part of the human race.

I believe that it is quite obvious that "racism" must be something very different than our vernacular use of this term. Accurate would be: to be a racist is not an attitude—but to be very seriously ill.

I can imagine that many are now surprised. Yes, of course, racism is hate. But this hate that we call "racism," is nothing else but self-hatred!

Before I go into further detail to explain the reason for this "self-hatred," let me first quote Dr. Stephan Lermer, who explains his research, "Prejudice and racism are always the results of endured violence, oppression, injury, exploitation, humiliation. Racists have created for themselves an option which allows the socially acceptable discharge of aggression. This works best when one joins a group that has endured the same suffering. One feels one's self among brothers, united by a common scapegoat, the enemy image, the Feindbild. Racists are unable to develop their psychosocial identity. They cannot harmonize their emotions, thoughts, desires, and actions. They use their hatred as a social defense mechanism. They need to strengthen their non-existent self-esteem at the expense of others. It is futile to try to counter them with facts or objectively correct arguments." (113)

That means, those who hate themselves (like Mark Fuhrman, for example) choose one of the "socially accepted targets" as an outlet, the Feindbild, (the German word Feindbild means enemy image) like women, Jews, homosexuals, Blacks, Hispanics and "Auslaender" (foreigner) which should simply serve as a red herring to divert from their self-hatred that otherwise would be "eating them from inside ," in the true sense of the word. (**A25) That means, the target of hate is nothing else but the camouflage for their self-hatred!

Now, imagine once again, Mark Fuhrman's psychiatric problems. Think of his group called "Men against Women ," (MAW) and his Anglo-Saxon-boy's-club, that makes his yearning for superiority transparent, (and so his obvious desperate fight against his feelings of inferiority) and then imagine whom he hates above all. Spontaneously, I remember Dr. Bernd Nitzschke's findings, "All men who join a hate group have repressed their desire for physical contact with the object of their hatred, which is socially taboo. To avoid this wish for symbiosis that has surfaced—namely a wish to unite symbiotically with the allegedly hated object of desires—the object of desire must become contemptible. Hatred of homosexuals, for example, is always the attempt to defend oneself against one's own homosexual desires and feelings." (115) I know that many people reacted sensitively about Johnny Cochran's comparing Adolf Hitler with Marc Fuhrman. Of course, Fuhrman is a little braggart and Hitler was a dangerous coward. But the illness itself, is indeed similar, and their hate is certainly the same.

Hate is a very strong emotion. As strong as love. And I am sure, that everybody knows the proverb, "Where there is no love there is no hate." And racism is hate. Unfortunately, the institution "Police" is the only place where such ill men can be "legally racists." That means: first of all, they will find like-minded all-boy-clubs (on a legal basis), or as Fuhrman puts it, "We were tight......we all knew what to say.". And they have, no doubt about it, the law on their side. Because they are the good guys, who have only one aim, to catch the bad guys. And they put their lives at risk. Whatever they do, they can excuse their actions with their duty as police officers. And the fine line between using one's authority for sadistic doings (excessive force) or necessary force, is difficult to prove unless someone had the luck Rodney King had.

However, whether they use the honorable profession of the police, or whether they use an official racist group as camouflage (and justification for hate), or whether they love hate radio, or love to write hate letters—the illness is the same. Let me take only two letters addressed to O.J. (he was already jailed) as an example of hate. What do we think is going on in such people's mind? Why would anyone in this world have feelings for someone whom he hasn't even met? But this is the case here. These letters are only an example of many examples; letters that show deep, deep emotions, tremendous feelings for an idol—for O.J.

I urge the reader to read the letters directed to O.J., by keeping Dr. Nitzschke's and Dr. Lermer's findings in mind: "...Now if something like this would only happen more often to Hollywood n----rs like say, Quincy Jones or Mr. Poitier, the world would be a better place. Ain't nothing worse than celebrity n----rs with money. The real problem you guys create, is that you have a habit of leaving behind your genetic traces in the form of mullato mutts. There should be a law passed to sterilize black males when they reach a certain income level. Let's face it, you guys didn't have the bucks, ain't no white woman would go near you. I mean what woman wants to have sex with a primitive jungle man? Goodby Juice, another coon in the can." (Karl K. King, Jacksonville, FL.) (116)

Another "anonymous" wrote "Filthy Murdering N—ER MOTHER F—KER S.O.B. COKE HEAD. But you're not the only worthless n—er in this country. Ninety-eight percent of you are UNTERMENSCH S—T. The Ugliest species on the planet. UGLY HAIR, like wire, pig ears, primate noses, bulbous lips, and your ugly blackness. Unconscionable, irresponsible, dysfunctional, immoral, degenerate, perverted mother f—kers. The whole race is of the same kind. You deserve the gas chamber. [Anonymous] Postmark: Belleville, Il." (117)

And Ron Hendrickson, Reno, NV writes, "I have a question for you and your buddy, A.C. What do you think of "white trash" bitches who like to f—k rich n—rs now?" I would not be surprised if this letter represents pretty close to Mark Fuhrman's views about O.J.. And I wouldn't be surprised to learn that Fuhrman was very attracted to Nicole Simpson. But would a racist go so far as to plant a bloody glove in order to bring a Feindbild down? His Othello, his O.J.? Whom he perhaps—aside from his fascination with Othello himself and the repressed desire for symbiosis —envied for the blond Valkyrie with her beautiful shoulders and bittersweet charm (whom he, too, must have hated)?

I doubt that Mark Fuhrman will confess in the Court of Law. But he confessed—compulsively, "I am the key prosecution witness in the trial of the century. If I go down and the glove goes out, their case goes bye-bye." (105) Here we can hear with his own voice, his abnormal desire for admiration! The yearning for triumph. But his abnormal desire for admiration is now satisfied, like Faye Resnick's through O.J.'s trial and its attention which I will discuss later in more detail.

His spokesperson, Anthony Pellicano, is excusing Fuhrman's lies in his testimony in front of the court (and the world,) that he hasn't said the N-word for ten years, that "he [Fuhrman] had a mental block."

If this is really the case that Fuhrman doesn't know details from his interviews with the screenwriter Laura McKinney anymore, and had therefore committed perjury, because he had, as he claims, a mental block, then he is, in fact, a case for a closed psychiatric institution. Since he has also forgotten the witness, Kathleen Bell, then it is also possible that he might have forgotten having planted the glove. Because of this psychological state of mind, is what he claims, in the final analysis.

I don't know whether Mark Fuhrman has in fact planted the glove, or not. Although many people are wondering why, Mark Fuhrman was always "the one" who was the first (to jump over the wall), or found something (blood in the Bronco, glove on an illogical place)—all alone. However, I can only say what "normal racists" are capable of. We know their racial slurs about women and all other well-known targets. And we know (at least since 1993) about their plans for a "race war in 1995 ."

We know from their religious "Militias" (which are racist groups with target Government)—one could say, they are groups similar to the Muslim Fundamentalists, only in this case they are Christian Fundamentalists. And we know that they are joined by Aryan Nations, Neo-Nazis, etc. How far these people, who suffer from pathological identity problems, will go is demonstrated about beating of homosexuals, the burning in 1993 of an African American, the killing of an African American woman as a "race traitor" because she colored her hair blonde and last but not least, the tragic Oklahoma bombing of May 1995. (118)

Regardless of the different targets, all these people have one thing in common: they suffer an inner hell, the chemistry of their 100 billion neurons in their mind is severely damaged from childhood on, and if the psychiatrist and medication can't do one's bit—then only hate can have them forget, at least for a couple of hours, their self-hatred. The same cause (that creates racists) is responsible for increasing violence, teenage suicide, disorders and phobias, and clinical depressions. Racists are one of the extreme forms of this illness. The next stage would then be schizophrenia (as Mark Fuhrman, the perfect metaphor, demonstrates).

But what is the reason for so much pain and inner hell? Why do some people, like for example Mark Fuhrman, suffer to such an extent, so that they believe there is only one way out of their inner hell—to "hate" another religion, skin color, gender, attitude, sexual orientation? But since there is not even a race other than a human race, what is then the true "Race Card?" Why would some people hate themselves in the first place, and then convert their self-hatred into hate? And why is this "racism" newest history, which means it didn't exist before 1000 B.C.? As I mentioned already, the true "Race Card" is the mother! Without racism between man and woman, that caused eighty generations ago, the "Breakdown of the Identification Phase with the Mother," there wouldn't exist phenomena that we call "racism." Do you remember the vital Identification Phase with the Mother that I have explained in connection with Eunice? Our forefathers and foremothers, who were peaceful and happy people, who never live outside the Laws of Nature, lived for 100,000 years according to nature. The Breakdown of this Identification Phase with the Mother (and so the origin of the root of almost all evils!) has its origin roughly 3,000 to (fortified) 2,500 years ago, because a group of men interfered with nature. It took place in the frame of the first men's movement in history, that had started somewhere in the Ida-mountains in Greece and made its way from there around the world. The Greek woman was the first who was enslaved, had no name of her own anymore, she was the first who was declared to be responsible for famine and natural disaster. The Greek woman was the first "guilty woman who is responsible for man's guilt" (original sinner) in this world and was considered to be, in Aristotle's words, "a vessel for the semen."

Unfortunately, the Greeks didn't know that their short-sighted triumph is connected to a larger and more serious psychological problem, and they didn't know, couldn't know about the importance of the mother for our societies—especially for the sons!

With the downfall of the mother, when the most important person in everybody's life became a slave, a servant, second class, the guilty party, then the family, the heart of society, became ill. Being a racist is nothing other than being the victim of a very personal, private tragedy, that takes place at the core of the family. As we have already discussed, the misconception in this world is, that most people believe that the father figure is the decisive factor for their children's well-being, and to set an example of "strength." As we discussed, many believe (because we are trained that way) that we should be discussing primarily the Identification Phase with the Father, especially if we are talking about the more jeopardized, the emotionally more vulnerable and problematic group—namely, the sons. But exactly this is not the case. In the contrary, it is against nature. And it is a misconception that causes violence, hate, and racism.

We believe in this misconception, that there must be someone in the family a "dominating father figure," who is feared and spanks to discipline the children (instead of discussing and understanding their view, too).We believe it because we are trained to believe in it. Our parents believed it, our grandparents believed it, our great grandparents believed it. And roughly further sixty to eighty generations before us believed the same. But this is just not right, as we can see from the result, according to a CNN documentary, "Racism is on its rise."

These kind of family values are new history and have been artificially created over the course of 3,000/2,500 years in the course of the first men's movement in history. The Greek cult figure and priest, Hesiod, one of the leading figures in the movement, created in the frame of the first men's movement in history, the idea of "the new race of man," (119) which developed over the centuries (and used force), as its alter ego, of course, "the new race of woman ." Which means, psychologists describe this new race of woman then, one hundred generations later in a documentary (August 1994): "She feels subconsciously second class and believes her domain is the kitchen." (120)

But we aren't that way by nature. We developed tremendously over the course of centuries , and we are all different. It is just not true that every boy is a young devil, and every girl has maternal instincts. Some women are fighters, and some men are fighters. Some men are more docile, as are some women. Some women are intellectual, as some men are, and some men are extroverts as some women are. Some men are shy, as some women are. Some women are courageous, as some men are.

There is no difference in our brains. There are only differences in our upbringing. And this "upbringing," and nothing else is the cause for identity problems of boys and girls alike. This simple word "upbringing" is the cause for an increase of 500% teenage suicide (female/male alike!) or for severe identity problems of girls who " would rather be boys," and boys "who would rather be girls." (**A26) This "upbringing" is responsible for the increase of 179% violence, hate and self-hatred, eating, panic, sleeping disorder, phobias and depressions, lack of self-esteem and self-confidence, pathological inferiority complexes (like Hitler and Fuhrman) and therefore pathological yearning for superiority, often psychosomatic illnesses,—and it is responsible for the illness "racism".

"But what is wrong with our upbringing? What is then the real cause for our increasing problems? Especially since so many different problems are interrelated together," many will certainly ask. As we discussed, the true "Race Card" is the mother itself! Yes, the mother is the cell of our increasing violence, depressions, and racism (self-hatred). But the mother is, in turn, also the cell of happiness, self-confidence, and accomplishments—if she loves herself and is, therefore, able to give her children strength, protection, love—and identity.

The mother is the most important part of the "factory" for our computer-chip—the mind. The little baby's brain that is only filled with basic human needs— eating, sleeping, sex, breathing, and drinking —and is totally dependent on mother's teachings, feelings, reactions, and paying attention to the little child. The brain will be filled via biochemical processes from day one on, slowly but surely with all sort of experiences and events. These experiences are primarily connected to feelings. The mother looks in baby's eyes. The baby is happy. The mother takes the baby in her arms. The baby is happy. The baby gets to eat. The baby is happy. The mother leaves the baby. The baby is unhappy. The mother doesn't pay attention to the baby. The baby is unhappy. The mother is sad. The baby is sad. The mother is unjust. The baby is confused. The mother abandons the baby. The baby suffers mortal terror.

And this goes on when the baby is a toddler, child, or student. Whatever the mother does, or does not do (!), baby's brain stores and absorbs. And often there are things that mothers do that baby's brain cannot digest. We call these moments "key experiences," that according to the child's mentality can grow even into a childhood trauma. Be it that the mother leaves the child to father's punishment, the "strong father figure" (which means he had to discipline the child), which the child should learn to respect and fear. Why would the mother need the "feared father figure" to discipline the children? Isn't she respected enough to discipline her children herself? Why create fear in the family at all? The family should be the safest place on earth. The ultimate protection, the nest.

Every event and every experience influences the brain via biochemical processes. Even the most insignificant event will leave its mark in one's brain. And how we feel about this or that-how we absorb and digest this or that, or what made us happy, gave us self-confidence, or confirmation to be outstanding, that's the way our personality and self-confidence is going to develop. We can compare these processes in the mind with the storing process in a computer chip. The computer chip will then "spit out," and repeat exactly the way it had been stored. That's similar with our minds. That means, it is only logical that a self-confident and thus happy mother, will make her child happy by contrast.

Or let me put it this way: As racists convert their self-hatred into hate, so do those thirty-eight percent of women who hate themselves into depressions, eating, panic and other disorders, or psychosomatic illnesses, etc.

An unhappy (and perhaps depressed) mother who plays a role that society dictates her and she doesn't like.

The saying of "quality time instead of quantity time" is just true. A mother who is happy with herself, her life, and her future, can make her children happy.

The mother decides (subconsciously and often unknowingly) whether her son will become successful and happy, or will end up like Mark Fuhrman, who struggled all his life to get a grip on his psychological problems.

The Psychology Professor, Joachim Seidl, once said: "It sounds foolish to say so, but every baby is born good." (123) And I thought of men like Mark Fuhrman, or Timothy McVeigh. And I felt sorry for them, pondering what might the father and mother have done to them? Nobody is born violent, (**A27) perverted, seething with hatred, full of depression, and certainly not a racist. No man would hate women by nature, and no woman would hate man by nature. And nobody is condemned to have identity problems.

Interestingly enough, psychologists, according to latest research, concluded that "boys suffer more [than girls] when the mother ignores them." (126) I have seen videotapes, and studied many mother/son relationships. I was stunned, but it was true. Boys indeed suffer much more than girls when the mother ignores them. They cry as if they had mortal terror. I studied many cases over the course of years, as well as the research that was available, because I also wanted to know, "what is it that is so extremely important" that the mother is responsible for her son's self-confidence to the extent that she is able to decide her child's fate and future?

Perhaps it is the most important feeling, for a baby to know that it is worthy of being loved. So that from there the computer chip in one's mind can repeat for one's entire life: "I am worthy of being loved, I am admired—I am worth a lot." And I realized that it is, in fact, true that people who love themselves, their bodies, their minds, their personalities, are capable of loving others. And this love for oneself—this starts with the mother—the first love in man's life.

But over the course of years and studying of many cases, I also believe that a child wants to get the confirmation from somebody whom she/he admires and respects. Because only from an admired authority, does the recognition carry weight.

A child realizes (or feels) very quickly the hierarchy ladder in a family, and which position one has. I have seen many cases that children, from a certain age on, rejected the mother as a role-model and didn't want to identify with her, because, for example, to stay with the mother "was weak," and a "mama's boy" even if the son loved the mother. The admired person was the father. He was the one who should pay attention to his heroic deeds. And his recognition carried weight. And the heroic deeds were almost exclusively of physical character. I often asked myself, how should such boys develop their strength and self-confidence in a computer and technology world? In a world where certainly not the shooting of the largest prey will earn laurels, or who can beat the neighbor's boy better—but ingenious ideas would indeed!

I am sure that if we would analyze Mark Fuhrman's relationship with his mother and father, we will have a similar pattern (psychogram) as it is valid for almost all racists, and as it was already with Adolf

Hitler's mother and father. Besides, that Adolf's mother considered herself despite marriage "to be Alois' servant," his father disciplined him sadistically, and he was beaten up almost every day. Mark's mother must have failed as a mother (like Adolf's), otherwise he wouldn't wouldn't hate women. But he does. Fuhrman's group "Men Against Women, " is in reality rather a cry of despair of a man with a wounded soul who went astray in this world, and whose only light at the end of the tunnel was to hate others and to forget himself.

It is interesting, that Hitler himself is *the* example par excellence, for this kind of societal problem, i.e. psychological misconception of women's "role" in society, that caused not only Adolf's psychological dilemma and certainly Mark Fuhrman's "psychiatric report that he is a racist" (127), but a lot of unhappy people around the world. The true "Race Card" was always the same, is the same, and will be the same. It is the result of racism between men and women—and the lack of the vital identification phase with the mother. (**A28)

If the identification phase with the mother doesn't take place positively, then as a consequence, parts of our brains will never be developed, or, a scientist says, they are lost forever. There is no doubt, this is what had happened to Adolf when he still was a little child. Or as Professor Joachim Seidl would say, "when he still was a baby that has been born good." His parents created this sort of creature we know, and that has developed far away from being a human. Via biochemical processes, he developed into a superiority maniac because of his pathological feelings of inferiority.

Adolf is the result especially of his mother and of course, of his father. The mother was too weak to protect him from the father. She, who accepted her second-class identity, believed - that's the way it was and that the strong father figure's job was to discipline the children and to tell her what to do. Adolf Hitler's father, Alois, was the dictator of the family. Everybody was subordinate to him. Hitler's mother, a former maid and domestic servant, was also not exactly someone with whom Adolf wished to identify with pride. Hitler biographer, Joachim C. Fest, explains, "She came to his father, Alois, as a housemaid and considered herself throughout her life to be, despite their marriage, Alois' servant and mistress." (128) However, Adolf, desperate, lost in the real world, began to flee into his fantasy world and to cling to the Germanic gods as the only support with which he could identify. Already at age eleven, little Adolf was crazy about the German gods and their history.

Like Fuhrman and every racist, Adolf was also a huge braggart. His schizoid personality and irrationality, are demonstrated by the following story. Adolf once bought a lottery ticket. Long before the day of the drawing, he had already spent, in his wildest dreams, the money that he had not even won. When the day of the drawing came, Adolf's ticket lost. He became furious and accused the state of "being fraudulent." (Hitler always seemed to need a scapegoat, if things didn't work out in his life). He had wanted to put into action his great plans with all the money he had already won in his dreams. (129)

The schizoid personalities of Adolf and Mark, are pretty much the same, with one difference. Fuhrman has, by contrast to Adolf's circumstances of six million jobless, desperate people who grabbed every straw, only the Trial of the Century. "If I go down, and the gloves go out, their case goes bye-bye," he brags. The lack of responsibility in the personality, the irrationality of such people, is also interesting. Fuhrman was, in my opinion, never an honorable police officer. He used this institution for his hate. Similar to Adolf's pathological hate against the Jews and his dream of the Germanic Reich, that was more important than the fate of millions of Germans and their future. Adolf lived Mark Fuhrman's principle, "If I go down"—then everybody goes down.

Again, hatred is always self-hatred. And self-hatred follows if the identification phase with the mother cannot be experienced positively. As I said, racism is new history. Since the first men's movement in history has prevailed and as a result, it is the Identification Phase with the mother that is in trouble. And it took a long time. It needed almost a thousand years to be really established in society, and it needed excessive force, that fortified from century to century. The Greek woman was the first, the next was the Roman woman who was enslaved, and was followed in the course of the centuries, by almost all countries around the world. Hate, i.e. racism against women in Europe, increased to the point, that thirty million female scientists who lived in the Middle Ages, were prosecuted and killed as "witches," although there has never existed a magician who would be able to fly through any air, or could make any sort of miracle.

These murdered women, whom we call today witches, were in reality experts on medical science. They were the doctors. They knew 103 different chemical and physical procedures of medical science—and of course, they knew the secret of birth control. The first execution of a woman scientist, knowledgeable in medicine and birth control, accused as a "witch" because she allegedly "ate up children," is documented in 1350. (130) The murderer was forced to stop this woman holocaust, because women in Europe were almost extinct. That means the ecological balance was in trouble. (131)

But even if the killing of women had to be stopped, the men's movement went on and on in its "own ways." For example, archeologists from the nineteenth and twentieth centuries falsified and embezzled the true history, inventions, and achievements of women so that all inventions were from then on made by men only. The psychological message did its bit. The majority of women and with the help of psychological group pressure got this message over the course of the centuries until she really believed in it and turned into a "good woman."

This way of thinking didn't really change until this very day. At least the majority believe that our societal concept would be all right indeed. If this wouldn't be the case, why would there then be any woman who says proudly, "Uh, giggle, giggle, I am a bitch." Why then would TV documentaries like "Gender War," "The Better Sex," "Are Women Inferior to Men?" exist after all and why would psychologists have to , "She [the woman] feels subconsciously second-class and believes, her domain is the kitchen." (132) And if everything was "all right" why would, according to statistics, thirty-eight percent of women hate themselves? (26) (*) Why would anybody in this world have any reason to hate oneself? Be it a Mark Fuhrman, an Adolf Hitler or a woman?

And why would "racism be on the rise?" (CBS) Because the sons of those women, who became the 38%thirty-eight percent statistics of self-hatred, don't know that they would be the only one in this world who could make their husband's dream come true: namely that "his" son will indeed become strong. But as long as it is not "their son"—as long their son is *his* son, he, "his son" will struggle all his life to overcome his feelings of "not being worthy," and resulting psychological problems and will yearn for outlets and artificial superiority.

In reality, they don't really hate themselves, they hate their "role" that society dictates for them or their body's image that includes the subconscious suggestion "you can't do it." And if you do, then you are a "career woman" a "feminist," or whatsoever. A role that often just doesn't fit their mind, which is sexless anyway. It is the *intellectual identity* that is sexless, that has nothing to do with gender, or sexual feelings, eros or desire— unless one either talks one's self into believing that it does. Sex is one of the basic human needs (eating, drinking, breathing, sleeping, sex) according to Maslow's pyramid (133) which is controlled by the old brain matter. Unfortunately, many people are not raised according to their intelligence and capability; we are still brought up according to our sex, or gender and its expectation.

Professor Jared Diamond (UCLA) states , "One might regard womanhood as the natural state of (hu)mankind." (134) As soon as the fetus takes the characteristics of a particular gender, the sexual gender organs of the other stop developing. All babies who have ever lived or will ever live, are as a principle, first female. Each fetus would naturally develop into a female.

However, I heard this kind of misconception again and again, simply because it is planted by our parents and grandparents in our minds, because their parents and grandparents did the same, and so on. Most of us are trained that way. We don't know that this is against nature, unnatural, artificial and the root of all evil. The root of violence and racism. "You are raising my son. You're at home—be happy about it," or "I gave you my sperm, you carried it out," and "I wanted you to have my baby," or even a woman blamed her unfaithful husband, "I bore your son." (135) Or even an intelligent person like Oprah Winfrey reminded a husband of his role as bread-winner, by saying "It was your sperm who made her egg, that created that child." (136) (**A29) These are all wrong ideas, that certainly cannot function in the world of the twenty-first century anymore. Because this is just not true. Was not, is not, will not.

And should not! It is not the man's sperm that made any egg or creates a child. (**30)

This is the real connection between our frightened observation that "Racism is on the rise!" Such wrong ideas are, like it or not, a reminiscence of the first men's movement in history, that started roughly 1000/800 B.C. in Greece, created severe identity problems in men and women alike and made from there its way around the world. Woman's history has been embezzled for hundreds of years, as well as in the eighteenth and nineteenth centuries (also around the world). But have history books been corrected? Not at all. Young girls in the 1990s still learn that women have not very much to do with all great inventions in this world. If, at all, then it was just chance. Girls (girls that will be one day mothers), from the "New York Humanistic High School,", who have the privilege to live in the 1990s, which is one of the best times in our history ever, expressed in a 1993 documentary, "[they] would rather be a man." (139) And again, it is not their body, that they don't love, it is the image that the body has—in their own family!

They don't know (and perhaps their parents don't know) that almost all great inventions have been made by women. From agriculture to architecture, an irrigation system to medicine, surgery to writing, mathematics to our today's modern religion. I can imagine that they don't know about embezzlements, alteration, falsification, forgery of historical evidence of events when it comes to women's achievement. But it was a Sumerian woman who invented the revolutionary writing in 3500 B.C. Another Sumerian woman invented mathematics, as well as the law, today's religion, the first school and the first teacher. This part of the world is our biblical "Garden of Eden." (the Sumerian word Aa'dan=Eden means grassland) And therefore, Sumeria is called "The Cradle of Civilization," after all.

Then, another neighboring island, that was lead by the Cretian women, who were for thousand of years the economic superpower of the entire Aegean Sea, due to their revolutionary inventions that allowed them to store their grain and to feed the entire region. They lived in luxury—but in peace. They developed Europe and are therefore called, "The Cradle of European Civilization." The Sumerian and the Cretian women are the most important, and some of the greatest inventors of all time, who invented almost all our basic inventions that allowed us to become what we have become today.

I know that there is a huge and rich history that needs to be told so that men and women will realize that they were always partners, namely two halves that makes one whole. They were never before in history enemies, who needed groups like "Men Against Women." But it would be impossible for me, to discuss the entire and interesting (true) history in this chapter, which will demonstrate what happened that "racism" originated after all, but which will be documented in my next book, *God Is A Handy Excuse*.

But even if I touch upon some important points only very short,—some facts are important for this book, in order that we can understand the connection, (and recognize the importance) between the

"Identification Phase with the Mother",—but on the other hand the enslavement of the mother, (and still in the 1990s feels "second class") as well as "racism" as a consequence (societal illness), which will be forever connected to the breakdown of the Identification Phase with the Mother. Due to this breakdown, which fortified in some centuries, and consequently, it was carried on from generation to generation. And so, in the course of 3,000/2,500 years, a new type of woman developed. A type that does not even exist by nature and that I named in my research work, "the good woman."

As I said, women (primarily the scientists and intellectuals) have been prosecuted for hundreds of years, and thirty million have been burned at stake. Their mortal terror to be chosen to be a "witch" must have grown to the extent that we cannot imagine, until she became, in fact , docile over the centuries. In short: Hundreds of years of mortal terror to be burned at the stake, developed a fear of death, so that women started to reduce themselves, play "the good woman" and—she started (due to biochemical processes over the course of hundreds of years of pressure and mortal terror) slowly but surely indeed to believe in the second class idea, which in turn caused biochemical processes.....

And of course, to survive, she accepted her role and fate, that her capacity and her world, i.e. "her domain" cannot be otherwise than the kitchen. This type is, as scientists call it, the result of one's "upbringing," (121) and means the biochemical processes that our first gods, mother and father cause in baby's mind. As I said, the Greek cult figure and priest, Hesiod, one of the leading figures in the first men's movement, called this insecure (and new) type of man "the new race of man," to which only the "new race of woman" would be adequate. The new race of woman ended up in a Germanic folktale, that we call (due to Walt Disney's beautiful animation of this cruel fairytale) with much tenderness, Cinderella, and the Prince. But the concept of Cinderella and the Prince is, not more and not less, the result of hundreds of years of racism between men and women, which is, in turn, mainly the root for identity problems and insecurity and therefore the cause for the epidemic of racism in general.

Be that as it may, I hope that people will understand why I took O.J. and Nicole and Mark as a metaphor. Scientists try for years to warn people around the world that "survival is a worldwide change of mind." (140) But what does it mean that we have to change our mind? It means that we have to change the culture, institutions, education, government, and religions. The anthropologist, Dr. Melvin Konner, speaks even of "mass extinction" and "self-destruction" if we can't change our minds worldwide. These are very harsh words—but they are unfortunately true. Professor John P. Holdren makes it even more clear. "If the human spirit of cooperation is not solved, nature will solve it for us in much less pleasant ways." (141)

And what do those scientists mean? They mean that our species might be one of the last generations on Mother Earth. That serious? That serious! And they made it very clear that only with the spirit of cooperation (and so getting the problems around the world under control) we will be able to survive. But the spirit of cooperation can only start at home. And only strong identities are able to cooperate. This is the mentality that can survive in a world of the twenty-first century. The world that in only fourteen years will have to deal with twice the population, namely with ten billion people. The twenty-first century will be a difficult world. It will be the world of overpopulation, increasing temperatures, rising sea levels, melting ice caps, threatened coastlines, crops and water supplies and intensified hurricanes. The world of the third millennium will be the world of solving problems. And these problems can only be solved with the spirit of cooperation caring for a World Community. And this spirit of cooperation starts at home.

The formula for the healing process around the world sounds very simple (and it is so difficult to realize 2,000 years misconception): if the mother is okay then the family is okay. If the mother subconsciously hates herself, then her offspring will do the same. But even if it's difficult, I personally believe, that we have to start somewhere...

I believe that the O.J. drama has gotten out of proportion. It's not even O.J.'s fault. It's the media's fault. They were and still are, in love with the Trial of the Century. But perhaps exactly this obsession with this fact-based soap opera will help to get the message out, and—will do justice to Nicole and Ron .

Eleonora De Lennart

Eleonora De Lennart, PhD, is an acclaimed scientific researcher, bestselling author, and entrepreneur. Her family originated from England (Lennard Dacre). She is the author of the groundbreaking thesis, *God Is A Handy Excuse,* as well as the groundbreaking discovery and bestseller, *The BioChemical Machine 2; Empowering Your Body Chemistry, The Night of the Scorpions, and Quinky—Destiny Dog.*

Eleonora De Lennart's research has been enthusiastically endorsed by notable members of the scientific community, including Professor Julian Jaynes, Princeton University, Professor Dr. Claus Leitzmann, UCLA, Professor Helmut Minne, M.D., University of Heidelberg, Dr. Kilmer McCully, AB, MD, MA (hon) Harvard University, and Dr. Sharon Y. Robinson, New Jersey Department of Health, to name just a few.

She has been featured in publications ranging from *Woman's World* and *First for Women* to *Petra*

Magazine as well as having made appearances on numerous radio and television shows.

Eleonora De Lennart is a member of the American Association of University Women as well as the American Society of Journalists and Authors, ASJA, New York. She lives with her husband in upstate New York.

You can find more stories such as this at www.bookstogonow.com

If you enjoy this Books to Go Now story please leave a review for the author on the site which you purchased the ebook. Thanks!

We pride ourselves with representing great stories at low prices. We want to take you into the digital age offering a market that will allow you to grow along with us in our journey through the new frontier of digital publishing.
Some of our favorite award-winning authors have now joined us. We welcome readers and writers into our community.

We want to make sure that as a reader you are supplied with never-ending great stories. As a company, Books to Go Now, wants its readers and writers supplied with positive experience and encouragement so they will return again and again.

We want to hear from you. Our readers and writers are the cornerstone of our company. If there is something you would like to say or a genre that you would like to see, please email us at inquiry@bookstogonow.com

FOOTNOTES/BIBLIOGRAPHY

For your information, we used two different "serial numbers" for the FOOTNOTES:

a) For the Footnotes with either statements or detailed explanations. These numbers are from A 1 until A 30

b) The numbers 1 to 141 (they are just in brackets and without letter) refer to direct statements of the protagonists mentioned in this book, taken from following books:

"Nicole Brown Simpson" by Faye Resnick and Mike Walker, Dove Books, 1994

"Raging Heart" by Sheila Weller

"OJ Simpson" by Don Davis, 1995

The Brown and Goldman family and others may have used the same (or similar) original statements taken from their memory and/or personally experienced events and/or personal interpretation of events.

[1][1]A1 (**) But what we call "an obsession with this case" is nothing but another one of our basic needs—identification with other living things. But this identification, in turn, depends on one's own nervous system. And the nervous system is dependent on your own childhood experiences with your family—brothers and sisters, teachers, friends, uncles and aunts— personal key experiences. The central nervous system is not reliable in judging criminal cases. It cannot be trusted to judge a person you don't personally know, and it cannot be trusted in a case like O.J.'s, if you weren't personally there when the murder took place. Because your judgment is dependent on your very personal world and experience. Or in scientific terms, as Professor Jaynes explains, this is "misleading identification based on physical chemistry, not on introspective psychology." Just take movies as an example. Often, we show more sensitivity to films than to real life, where we react more brutally and thoughtlessly. We even identify actors with the roles they are playing; we equate the characters they play with their real-life personas (though? here can sometimes be a prodigious difference). We are transported by something that is written and directed by other people. Lights, music—everything is fantasy. But we shake, we sweat, we get angry, we feel terror, we get stomach cramps—we even cry. Even if we want to stop for shame, we cannot control our tears.

A2 (*) According to latest statistics, 38 % of American women. (26)

A3 (**) I am sure that this is no longer the case in many cases, but according to my studies, this is the case with the majority. Or as psychologists in a CNN documentary evidently explain, "women feel subconsciously second-class and believe their domain is the kitchen. (27) There is still the excuse "woman is getting the babies." This is true, but they aren't getting babies their entire life and every year, that would disqualify her forparticipating intellectually and actively in society.

A4 (**) Depression is the repressed aggression that people feel toward other people or situations from childhood, but that people don't dare to express–and so turn it against themselves.) Therefore, often depressed people subconsciously (intentionally) create conflicts to involve a guilty party (in this case O.J.) because then they are "allowed," so to speak, because there is a "guilty party," to live out their repressed violent anger.

A5 (**) But as Professor Joachim Seidl said, "Every baby is born good." And everybody is born to be a winner. It's up to us to make this decision somewhere in life and to work on it. Also, later in life and even if we weren't that lucky with our parents. At a certain point in life, we are no longer dependent on them, and should not even blame them. We should start and make up for the lost years (even if it is hard) and work to become the person who we want to be and who we really are.

A6 (**) Test yourself: Is the glass of beer for you still half full, or already half empty? You can train yourself to change this attitude in your subconscious via biochemical processes—if you want (first) and with perseverance (secondly). I have developed a method of how you can help yourself, with the "bottle." You put yourself into the bottle and try to open it by yourself, and allow yourself to fly as far as you want. Due to biochemical processes, you can allow yourself (by saying the right code words, "I allow myself to be successful, I allow myself to be happy.") every day— every day!—"to become successful and happy" to overcome the subconscious "success prohibition." But it is much easier

to do it with the help of a psychologist, i.e. psychotherapist, who knows exactly how to help you.
A7 (**) Professor Joachim Seidl is a Member of the Society for Psychotherapy, Psychosomatic and Depth Psychology, and Professor of the Academy for Psychoanalysis and Psychotherapy.

A8 (**) A *Washington Post* article represents the view of the majority by comparing O.J. to the classic Shakespeare story of Othello, "a brooding Moor in obsessive and ultimately fatal, love with a white woman." And O.J.'s reaction, "what they're saying is that my life is about rage, envy, jealousy, and desire. I'm being portrayed as a wife-abuser and a violent person. This is not fair and is untrue." (53) Good, everybody in O.J.'s shoes, guilty or innocent, will react the same way and will say "this is not fair and is untrue." Shakespeare's Othello is an important, physically imposing symbol of leadership and celebrity, in his 17th Century society, who is black. His wife, Desdemona, is fair and beautiful, and the embodiment of the aristocracy of that same society, and is white. Shakespeare's triangle includes Iago, the traitor, and manipulator, a man with a very bad character, who persuaded Othello that his loving wife had betrayed him. In 1603, there was no doubt in anyone's mind that Othello could have only one idea in his mind: "If I can't have her, nobody can."

*(A9) I can vividly imagine, that neither Faye nor Nicole told Ron about their financial problems, (**) and that they were struggling themselves tomaintain the lifestyle to which they were accustomed. They played their roles perfectly.

A10 (*) During my research for this book, I interviewed some members of my family who are the fourth generation to live in Beverly Hills. As socialites with insider knowledge (and their help to make this book possible), I was able to complete the puzzle as perfectly as possible. My conclusions are based on such knowledge. I was often not allowed to reveal details to their full extent because of security reasons. Nobody wanted to end up like Nicole and Ron, and as Johnny Cochran said on October 4, 1995 (56) "....where a good friend of hers [Resnick] has been killed in another city in California."

A11 (**) And this would be one of the points, among others, for Resnick's guilty conscience, because Ron didn't know, he couldn't know.

A12 (**) "I'm going to have to ask you to leave," said the head of security at the disco club, The Gate. "Camille doesn't want you back here." (65) Nicole, loyal as she was to Faye, left with her, though only Faye Resnick had been asked to leave.

A13 (*) but she had only $20,000 left (according to her own statement)

A14 (**) Accidentally or not, Istanbul is one of the drug paradises in this world

A16 (**) "I decided not to make my life a no-win situation. I knew there were white people who would always see me as black, and black people who would see me as not black enough," says O.J. Simpson in his book. And he goes on, "I decided not to do what I wanted to do and not let other people define my life. I would do my best with my abilities, and never allow my race to be used as a weapon against me." (95)

A17 (**) However, the admission of guilt is interpreted by many from the question that was raised by the detectives about taking a polygraph test. O.J. answered, "Eventually I will do it—but I had weird thoughts." Of course, he was afraid. One month later, on July 15, 1994, O.J. did offer to take the polygraph test, but only on the condition that it be admitted as evidence at the trial, regardless of the outcome.

A18 (**) Tom Lange asked, "Excuse me again. She [Nicole] didn't get any threatening phone calls?" O.J. denied this and said "not at all." He could have maintained that Nicole had in fact received such threatening phone calls in order to protect himself. The legal expert, Vincent Bolliosi, for example, is stating in a *Hard Copy* interview, "He could have said there were all types of threats, she told me about that." (97) O.J. admitted during this interrogation, "For me it was a big problem, I loved her, I didn't want us to separate. I always had problems with her. You know, I—I um....That's—that's our relationship, it has been a problem relationship." Vincent Bollioso stated, "If he were guilty, he would not admit that the breaking up was his part." (97)

A19 (**)The criminal lawyer, Gerry Spence, speaking from his personal experience with the FBI, said, "You can bet that they will find the evidence they need." Another famous lawyer, Roy Black, left no doubt—if even one milligram of blood were missing from the vial then there's a "big hole."(101) Professor Alan Dershowitz has given several interviews explaining his research over the last twenty-five years in cases of police and D.A. conspiracy. He concluded that the police do indeed lie and commit perjury. (102) Professor Dershowitz is saying that as soon as the police find the man they think is guilty, they do everything necessary to get a guilty verdict at the trial. They are worried more than anything that defense lawyers will think up some trick to let the criminal go free.

A20 (**) "I don't believe for one moment there was a deliberate, conscious conspiracy on the part of 6, 8, 10, 12,

14 police officers and criminalists," stated the Pittsburgh forensic expert and pathologist Cyril Wecht, Ph.D. But on the other hand, Dr. Cyril Wecht is astonished at Vannatter "taking a tube of blood twenty-one miles away and holding on to it there for some hours?" (103) (**) Dr. Wecht tells about his own experience dealing with police and prosecution. "Don't assume that the prosecution and police in America are wonderful." And moreover, he says, "I believe that Vannatter made a serious boo- boo, and why he took the blood out there, I'm not sure I can understand that."

A21 (*) Adolf's family (on both his father's and mother's side) came from a poor, out-of-the-way area located between the Danube river and the Bohemian border. This local population was a thoroughly rustic one, interrelated for generations as the result of incest. Many of Hitler's family members were mentally impaired as the result of incest.

A22 (**) Considering Adolf Hitler's psychiatric problems (who could never have survived in real life) I am not surprised about his yearning for Germanic gods. It is known that he and his SSmen established an inner circle with a religious cult—Germanic gods. (109) Adolf Hitler is the "Father of the Aryan Syndrome." No doubt about it. But never did and never will exist such a thing like a blond and blue-eyed Aryan. Aryans are members of Indian tribes and/or Persians (Iran). Aryans are most certainly not Germanic, and cannot have anything to do with Germanic gods. Because the Germanics (i.e. whole Europe) didn't have originally male gods at all. The Europeans had only goddesses, unlike in other cultures, like Egypt, Sumeria, Babylonia, Asia, and India where the goddess always had her hero-god, hero-king, or hero-son. That means, the "sun" sign (the swastika) is in all cultures the sign of the hero, (often called sun god) and consequently cannot have its origin in Germany, but in India, or Asia.

A23 (***) Albinism is a rare hereditary condition in which the body has no tyrosine, one of the enzymes that form the pigment melanin, normally found in the skin, hair, and eyes.

 A24(**) Different skin colors just indicate the stage of either active pigmentation or degenerated pigmentations due to climatic changes. All human beings have pigmentation granules in their skin to protect them from deadly ultraviolet rays. In some people, this pigmentation activity was maintained more strongly, and they retained their original color, while in others it degenerated due to climatic changes, and the skin became light. All babies are light-skinned at birth, and they usually have blue, or at least light-colored, eyes, because their pigmentation granules still have not developed a chemical reaction to the effects of the sun. Only after several days, weeks or months, does the baby's skin develop color, in keeping with the evolved protective mechanism of its parent or one of its parents. (112)

 **(A25) And if we go now, again, through the list of scapegoats, (Jews, women, homosexuals, Blacks, Hispanics) we can see that the only group that remains not to be hated, are those whom they hate more than anything in this world: themselves!

A26 (**) Latest research shows that hundred of thousands of normal married men are cross-dressing, wearing women's dresses, to escape the stress of the "role" that society demands from them as "a man." In some cases, men are having an operation to become a woman. But what they really want is, the "role" of a woman, which they consider to be less stressful. (122)

A27 (*) But what can we expect if even in July 1994, a psychologist (124) who is supposed to be an expert with degrees and credentials, states in a TV interview that I recorded, "Children are becoming violent, and are developing insecurity because they are raised by a single parent, the mother." By the way, we have not even analyzed what it means, in 1995, to be strong. Given the fact that we don't need to hunt animals on a daily basis anymore, to have something to eat, I believe that the concept of strong should be more modernized and put into realistic terms. And I mean by that: today it is the mind that is strong. (or should be strong. Because from our little computer chip, develop self-confidence, self-love, and happiness).

 A27 (**) The excuse that, we are "a violent species" is also wrong. We are not the "Killer Ape," as it has been maintained for twenty-seven years by archeologists. Yes, we carry still the genes of Homo erectus in us. But Homo erectus was anything but a killer ape. Both women and men hunted only from time to time. They were peacefully and simply, gatherers who mainly cracked bones left behind by the beasts of prey to eat the marrow. (125) We are a peaceful species by nature. There is no doubt about it. Violence, perversion, and racism are originally not our nature.

A28 (**) I have studied 3000 cases of young men who all had a similar pattern of problems with their parents, and suffered abnormal inferior complexes and self-hatred.

A29 (**) The parents— together—create a child, as our forebears for thousands of years, did and lived together peacefully in ultimate partnership until 1000 B.C. happily ever after! And this is the only way for the future.

A30 (**) "When it comes to describing fertilization, biologists have got it all wrong. The egg is no passive lady-in-waiting. A wastefully huge swarm of sperm weakly flops along, a few sperm end up close to an egg. As they mill around, the egg selects one and reels it in, pinning it down in spite of its efforts to escape," explains the scientist David H. Freedman (137) "The gigantic hardy egg yanks this tiny sperm inside, distils out the chromosomes and sets out to become an embryo." Moreover, he says "Or would you have put it differently? Until very recently, so would most biologists. For decades they've been portraying sperm as intrepid warriors battling their way to an aging, passive egg that can do little but await the sturdy victor's final, bold plunge." "Men link potency to strong sperm," Emily Martin says. "You'd like your sperm to be like you, so no wonder everyone believed sperm were torpedos." From the early 1970s on, studies of the sperm and eggs of many species, have revealed that molecules released by the egg are critical to guiding and activating the sperm; that is, they trigger the sperm to release proteins that help it adhere to the egg. In fact, the egg might just as well be called "eager" as "passive." Among many species of lizards, insects, some crustaceans, and even turkeys, the egg doesn't always wait for the sperm's arrival. It can begin dividing without fertilization, and females can reproduce without sperm at

www.ingramcontent.com/pod-product-compliance
Lightning Source LLC
Chambersburg PA
CBHW071943150726
47999CB00001B/297